THE MICROWAVE
FRUIT & VEGETABLE
COOKBOOK

THE MICROWAVE FRUIT & VEGETABLE COOKBOOK

Val Collins

DAVID & CHARLES
Newton Abbot   London   North Pomfret (Vt)

Acknowledgements

I should like to thank Kate Pike and Fiona Waddell for all their spare time and assistance in testing the recipes and preparing the food for photography. To Thorn EMI Major Domestic Appliances Ltd, I offer my grateful thanks for supplying Tricity and Moffat microwave cookers and assisting with the photography.

Colour photography by John Plimmer, RPM Photographic, Havant. Line illustrations by Evelyn Bartlett.

With grateful thanks to my husband for his guidance and understanding, to my family for being my greatest fans, to my colleagues and friends for their patience and to Jack Angell of David & Charles for his encouragement.

British Library Cataloguing in Publication Data

Collins, Val
    The microwave fruit and vegetable cookbook.
    1. Cookery (Fruit)
    2. Microwave cookery
    I. Title
    641.6′4   TX811

ISBN 0-7153-8199-7
Library of Congress Catalog Card Number 81-65958

© Text Val Collins 1981   1986

© Colour illustrations Thorn EMI Major Domestic Appliances Ltd 1981   1986

First published 1981

Second impression 1986

Colour separations by Duplichrome Ltd, Birmingham
Typeset by Western Printing Services Ltd, Bristol
Printed in The Netherlands
by Smeets Offset BV, Weert
for David & Charles Publishers plc
Brunel House   Newton Abbot   Devon

Published in the United States of America
by David & Charles Inc
North Pomfret Vermont 05053 USA

Contents

Introduction

For me, fruits and vegetables which have been cooked by microwave are cooked to perfection, looking and tasting better than those cooked by any other method. Gone are the times of soggy, overcooked, tasteless vegetables which do absolutely nothing to please the eye, let alone the palate. With the advent of the microwave cooker, fruits and vegetables take on a fresher, brighter appearance and add a new dimension to the 'meat-and-two-veg' syndrome of our daily meal.

In bygone days the wealthy often consumed large quantities of meat and game each day, whilst the poor relied on the few available vegetables to supplement their meagre diet. Onions, leeks and cabbages were the most popular, but dried peas, beans and other lentils were also used. Herbs and the knowledge of their use were essential to the cook and the varieties grown far exceeded the few that are most common today. Spices, dried fruits and almonds provided the 'sweet course', but as sugar became more readily available fruit desserts and puddings were gradually introduced into the menu. Before deep freezing, the first spring fruits and vegetables came as a welcome relief from the monotony of the winter varieties. But in time, a greater selection of fruits and vegetables was brought from other countries, made available by improvements in food processing, quick-drying, deep freezing and refrigerated transportation.

Fruits and vegetables contain most of the nutrients, vitamins and minerals required by the human body and with endless varieties from which to choose and ways in which they may be served, can provide us with a large proportion of our daily food requirements. Prepared and cooked correctly, they enhance and improve almost any food whether they are served as part of a main dish or as an accompaniment to a meal.

In more recent years, considerable research has been carried out into methods of cooking fresh fruits and vegetables to retain their maximum vitamin content and flavour. With all its advantages, surely the microwave cooker must top the list with its speed in cooking enhancing the flavour, texture and colour of fruits and vegetables probably more than any other cooking method.

Any fruits or vegetables picked whilst young and tender barely need cooking to make them nourishing and delicious to eat. Commercially grown produce is usually harvested days before being sold in the shops but, when cooked by microwave, even these fruits and vegetables have a flavour and freshness which may be compared with those grown at home. In the microwave, fruits and vegetables are cooked in their own juices, requiring very little additional liquid or butter to bring out their full flavour – particularly good for slimmers. Reheating too is most successful as there is no drying out or loss in quality, which means that vegetables can be cooked in advance to be quickly reheated later after the main dish has been prepared.

This book contains a selection of my favourite fruit and vegetable recipes, to help microwave cooks expand their skills in the world of microwave cookery and produce meals for the enjoyment of their families and friends.

A selection of dishes for a cold buffet
1 *Celeriac Salad (page 55)*
2 *Beetroot in Soured Cream (page 46)*
3 *Leeks Vinaigrette (page 72)*
4 *Mushrooms à la Grecque (page 79)*
5 *Sweetcorn and Tuna Flan (page 60)*
6 *Avocado Ring Mould (page 36)*

The microwave cooker

The design of microwave cookers varies between the different manufacturers' models, but they are all similar in appearance and the basic principles

of microwave cooking are the same. Before beginning to use the microwave cooker, it is important to know how it operates and to read and understand all the facts given in the manufacturer's instructions with particular reference to the use of the correct utensils and general microwave cooking techniques. With the introduction of the variable power or selector control there is a greater flexibility and control of the cooking speed which may be compared with the equivalent of conventional oven settings. With many food items this is unnecessary but can be invaluable for those foods or dishes which may benefit from longer, slower cooking.

Different manufacturers portray the variable power settings on the control panels of their models in different ways. It is useful to compare these in chart form to enable you to adapt the cooking times given in this book to suit your particular model, but do check your microwave cooker instructions with reference to settings related to the percentage and power inputs.

Variable power settings and time chart

Descriptions of settings	1 KEEP WARM LOW	2 SIMMER MEDIUM/LOW	3 STEW	4 DEFROST MEDIUM	5 BAKE MEDIUM/HIGH	6 ROAST	7 FULL/HIGH NORMAL
Approximate percentage % input	25%	30%	40%	50%	60%	75%	100%
Approximate power input (watts)	150W	200W	250W	300W	400W	500W	650W
Cooking time (minutes)							
1	4	$3\frac{1}{4}$	$2\frac{1}{2}$	2	$1\frac{3}{4}$	$1\frac{1}{4}$	1
2	8	$6\frac{3}{4}$	5	4	$3\frac{1}{4}$	$2\frac{3}{4}$	2
3	12	10	$7\frac{1}{2}$	6	5	4	3
4	16	$13\frac{1}{4}$	10	8	$6\frac{3}{4}$	$5\frac{1}{4}$	4
5	20	$16\frac{3}{4}$	$12\frac{1}{2}$	10	$8\frac{1}{4}$	$6\frac{3}{4}$	5
6	24	20	15	12	10	8	6
7	28	$23\frac{1}{4}$	$17\frac{1}{2}$	14	$11\frac{3}{4}$	$9\frac{1}{4}$	7
8	32	$26\frac{3}{4}$	20	16	$13\frac{1}{4}$	$10\frac{3}{4}$	8
9	36	30	$22\frac{1}{2}$	18	15	12	9
10	40	$33\frac{1}{4}$	25	20	$16\frac{1}{2}$	$13\frac{1}{4}$	10

For times greater than 10 minutes simply add the figures in the appropriate columns
These figures are intended as a guide only as much depends on the temperature, density and thickness of the food and the shape and size of the cooking container

Microwave users with models which have one variable setting only (this may be marked defrost or medium) can also use the time chart as a guide to indicate the extra time required when reheating or cooking on this lower setting. Advice on cooking times is given in each recipe and all cooking is carried out on 'normal', 'full' or 'high' settings unless otherwise stated. Recipes in this book were tested in a model with a power input into the oven cavity of 650 watts. The wattage of your own cooker may be higher or lower than this in which case the cooking time must be decreased for the higher rated models and increased for the lower rated ones. In addition to this, cooking times can vary slightly between models with the same rated input. Therefore, try out a few of the recipes comparing the actual cooking times with the recommended cooking times, and remember to adjust accordingly for the other recipes throughout the book. For example, a recommended cooking time of 10 min in a microwave cooker with a power output of 650 watts, would need to be adjusted to approximately 12–13 min for a 500 watt model and to 8–9 min for a 700 watt cooker. However, remember that this is dependent upon the type and temperature of the food being cooked and the container being used; in addition, shorter cooking times need less adjustment and longer cooking times will require slightly more.

Utensils

One of the advantages of microwave cooking is that foods may be cooked and served in the same dish. Also owing to the fact that heat is only produced within the food itself nothing burns on, so containers are generally easier to clean and food tends not to stick.

Microwave energy is reflected from metal which means that aluminium, aluminium foil, tin, copper and stainless steel containers must not be used. However microwave energy passes through glass, pottery and china and so, provided that they have no metal trim, they are all excellent containers when cooking in the microwave.

To the new microwave user, I normally recommend sorting through the containers and dishes already available before embarking on buying new ones. Quite often it is possible to improvise, and most cupboards have an assortment of suitable ovenproof glass or pottery bowls, pie dishes, casseroles and flan dishes. Roasting bags and boiling bags are ideal for cooking some foods as they can be easily shaken or turned over to stir the contents during the cooking. Remember, however, that the wire ties supplied with some makes must not be used. Rubber bands or string ties make suitable alternatives and the bag should be tied loosely to allow some steam to escape.

Special microwave containers

There is now a wider choice of special microwave cooking containers and dishes available on the market, but a selection would depend on your needs and requirements. Some of these utensils are intended for conventional cooking as well as microwave and others are suitable for both microwave and the freezer, which are added advantages.

Browning dishes

These are specially designed for use in the microwave cooker. In appearance they are normal glass, ceramic or pyroflam dishes but have a special tin oxide coating on the base. When the dish is preheated in the microwave cooker, the base absorbs microwave energy and gets very hot. Food such as steak, chicken portions, sausages, bacon or chops are placed onto the hot base which sears the outside of the food, similar to grilling or frying, whilst microwave energy cooks the food. Browning dishes are not generally required in fruit or vegetable cookery but can be used in some recipes which require a light 'frying' application, for example when browning onions or when cooking 'oven chips'.

Paper

Kitchen paper may be used in the microwave to absorb moisture when reheating or cooking pastry items. Either the food can be placed on a layer of kitchen paper or alternatively a piece may be placed lightly over the top of the dish during the heating period.

Aluminium foil

If you notice during a defrosting, cooking or heating process that part of the food is overcooking, perhaps at an outside edge, it is possible to mask this part of the food from the microwave energy with a small, smooth piece of aluminium foil. However, the foil must not be allowed to touch the interior sides or back of the oven cavity, and it is advisable to check with the manufacturer's instructions with reference to the use of aluminium foil in your particular model.

Covering foods

When cooking conventionally, lids on dishes or saucepans assist in food heating through more quickly; it is the same when cooking in the microwave. Whether a lid on the casserole dish is used or food is covered with cling wrap, the steam is trapped inside and this will enable even and slightly faster results to be obtained. Covering food also allows minimal liquid to be used and ensures no flavour loss.

Preparing and cooking

The preparation of fruits and vegetables for cooking in the microwave is virtually the same as if cooking them conventionally and, as with all forms of cooking, age and thickness will affect the cooking times.

For faster, more even cooking in the microwave, cut fruits and vegetables into small even pieces. If being cooked whole in their skins, choose uniform sizes and the skins should be pricked or scored to prevent them bursting. Corn on the cob may be wrapped in greaseproof paper or left with the husk on during cooking. Arrange the whole fruits or vegetables evenly in a dish or on the cooker shelf and turn them over halfway through the cooking period. Place more delicate vegetables such as asparagus tips or broccoli spears in a dish with the more tender parts towards the centre. When 'boiling' potatoes it is usually better to cook them in their skins with a little added water and to remove the skins, if required, after cooking. Some kinds of potatoes cook extremely well either scraped or peeled, but some varieties tend to turn black during cooking in the microwave. Minimal liquid or butter is required and a guide to the quantities is given in the cooking chart. The amount of liquid used may be altered to suit individual preferences, but the cooking time should be altered accordingly. The cooking water should be salted to taste (up to $\frac{1}{4} \times$ 5ml tsp/$\frac{1}{4}$tsp) before adding the vegetables. Salt sprinkled directly onto the food can toughen it and tends to draw out the natural juices which are then thrown away with the cooking water.

Fruits and vegetables which are normally cooked in water should be covered to prevent them drying out when cooking. Stir or shake the food to distribute the heat and moisture during the cooking period. When this is not possible, turn the dish although, as already mentioned, this is not always necessary if a microwave cooker with a turntable is used.

Roasting bags, boiling bags or casserole dishes can all be used as cooking containers for vegetables. Roasting or boiling bags should only be loosely sealed to allow some steam to escape, and if a dish is covered with clingfilm, this should be pierced with the pointed end of a sharp knife to prevent steam building up inside. Allow vegetables to stand for 3–5 min at the end of the

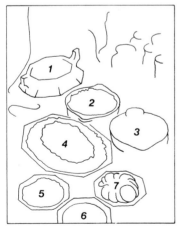

1 *Lentil Curry (page 75)*
2 *Banana Salad (page 38)*
3 *Aubergine Salad (page 34)*
4 *Okra Curry (page 84)*
5, 6, 7 *Curry accompaniments*

cooking time to finish cooking and develop their full flavour. This also enables them to remain hot whilst a complete meal is being served. Test whether cooked after the least amount of time shown on the chart – vegetables should be crispy tender but if preferred softer, just increase the cooking time by a few minutes.

Fruit should be sprinkled with sugar, cooked in a roasting bag or boiling bag and checked regularly to make sure it does not overcook. When it is important that the fruit pieces do not break, cook them in a covered casserole with a little liquid and increase the cooking time accordingly. Alternatively, cook them more slowly on a defrost or medium setting.

Remember that quantity will affect cooking times – allow up to $\frac{1}{2}$ extra time when doubling the amount to be cooked. When cooking an item such as a jacket potato, one potato weighing 100–150g (4–5oz) will take 5–6 min, two will take 7–9 min and three will take 10–11 min and so on.

Vegetable cooking chart

Vegetable and quantity	Preparation	Amount of salted water to be added	Cooking time in minutes on NORMAL, FULL OR HIGH
artichokes, jerusalem 450g (1lb)	peel and cut into even-sized pieces	4 × 15ml tbsp (4tbsp) or 25g (1oz) butter	8–10
asparagus 225g (8oz)	trim and leave whole	2 × 15ml tbsp (2tbsp)	thin spears 6–8 thick spears 8–10
aubergines 450g (1lb)	wash, slice, sprinkle with salt and leave for 30 min, rinse	2 × 15ml tbsp (2tbsp)	8–10
beans, broad 450g (1lb)	remove from pods	3 × 15ml tbsp (3tbsp)	8–10
beans, french 450g (1lb)	wash and cut	2 × 15ml tbsp (2tbsp)	8–10
beans, runner 450g (1lb)	string and slice	2 × 15ml tbsp (2tbsp)	8–10
beetroot 450g (1lb)	peel and slice	2 × 15ml tbsp (2tbsp)	7–8
225g (8oz) whole	prick skin, wrap in clingfilm		12–15
broccoli 450g (1lb)	trim, cut into spears	2 × 15ml tbsp (2tbsp)	8–12
brussels sprouts 450g (1lb)	wash, remove outer leaves and trim	2 × 15ml tbsp (2tbsp)	8–10
cabbage 450g (1lb)	wash and shred finely	2 × 15ml tbsp (2tbsp)	8–10
carrots 225g (8oz)	*new* wash, scrape and cut into strips or leave whole, depending on size	2 × 15ml tbsp (2tbsp)	7–10
	old scrape or peel and slice	,,	7–10
cauliflower 675g (1½lb)	wash and cut into florets	4 × 15ml tbsp (4tbsp)	10–11
450g (1lb) whole	trim outside leaves, wash	,,	10–11

celery 350g (12oz)	wash, trim and slice	3 × 15ml tbsp (3tbsp)	10–12
corn on the cob 2 × 250g (8oz)	wash and trim	4 × 15ml tbsp (4tbsp) *or* 40g (1½oz) butter	6–8
courgettes 450g (1lb)	wash, trim and slice	–	8–10
leeks 450g (1lb)	wash, trim and slice	2 × 15ml tbsp (2tbsp)	7–10
marrow 450g (1lb)	peel, cut into 2cm (¾in) rings, remove seeds and quarter the rings	2 × 15ml tbsp (2tbsp)	8–10
mushrooms 225g (8oz)	peel or wipe or wash	2 × 15ml tbsp (2tbsp) of stock *or* 25g (1oz) butter	5–6
okra 450g (1lb)	wash, trim, sprinkle with salt, leave for 30 min, rinse	2 × 15ml tbsp (2tbsp) *or* 25g (1oz) butter or oil	8–10
onions 225g (8oz)	peel and slice	2 × 15ml tbsp (2tbsp) *or* 25g (1oz) butter or oil	5–7
parsnips 450g (1lb)	peel and slice	2 × 15ml tbsp (2tbsp)	8–10
peas 225g (8oz)	remove from pods	2 × 15ml tbsp (2tbsp)	8–10
potatoes, new, in their jackets 450g (1lb)	wash thoroughly	2 × 15ml tbsp (2tbsp)	10–12
potatoes, old, in their jackets 450g (1lb)	wash and scrub thoroughly, dry and prick skins	–	10–12
spinach 450g (1lb)	break up thicker stalks, wash thoroughly	–	6–8
spring greens 450g (1lb)	break up thicker stalks, wash and shred	2 × 15ml tbsp (2tbsp)	8–10
swedes 450g (1lb)	peel and dice	2 × 15ml tbsp (2tbsp)	6–7
tomatoes 450g (1lb)	wash and halve, place in shallow dish and cover with lid or clingfilm	–	6–8
turnips 450g (1lb)	peel and dice	2 × 15ml tbsp (2tbsp)	8–10

Fruit cooking chart

Fruit and quantity	Preparation	Cooking time in minutes	
		NORMAL, FULL OR HIGH	DEFROST OR MEDIUM
cooking apples 450g (1lb)	peel, core and slice, sprinkle with sugar to taste	6–8	11–15
apricots 450g (1lb)	stone and wash, sprinkle with sugar to taste	6–8	11–15
peaches 4 medium sized	stone and wash, sprinkle with sugar to taste	4–5	7–8
pears 6 medium sized	peel, halve and core; dissolve 75g (3oz) sugar and a pinch of cinnamon in a little hot water, pour over the pears	8–10	15–20
plums, cherries, damsons, greengages 450g (1lb)	stone and wash, sprinkle with sugar to taste and add grated rind of ½ lemon	4–5	7–8
rhubarb 450g (1lb)	trim, wash and cut into short lengths; add 100g (4oz) sugar and grated rind of 1 lemon	7–10	14–20
soft fruits 450g (1lb)	top and tail currants, hull the berries; wash well and add sugar to taste	3–5	6–10

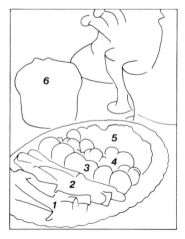

1 *Buttered Parsnips (page 92)*
2 *Glazed Carrots (page 54)*
3 *Glazed Turnips (page 117)*
4 *Glazed Onions (page 86)*
5 *Potatoes Duxelles (page 104)*
6 *Raspberry Soufflé (page 108)*

Blanching and freezing

Gardeners will be delighted with the ease of blanching by microwave as small quantities can be picked in peak condition and immediately blanched and frozen.

Fruits

Of the fruits, only apples, pears and rhubarb require blanching, although pears and rhubarb are best frozen cooked or in a purée form. Soft fruits can

be spread onto trays for open freezing or they may also be puréed – either cooked or uncooked. Fruits required in slices or whole may be packed in dry sugar or in a sugar syrup which lengthens the storage life by protecting against oxydisation. The discoloration of fruits such as apples, pears and peaches can be prevented by preparing quickly and placing them in a solution of 500 milligrams of ascorbic acid in 550ml (1pt) of water. Alternatively, 250 milligrams of ascorbic acid crystals or a squeeze of lemon juice may be added to 275ml ($\frac{1}{2}$pt) sugar syrup, using 100g (4oz) sugar to 275ml ($\frac{1}{2}$pt) water for a thin syrup, or 275g (10oz) sugar to 275ml ($\frac{1}{2}$pt) water for a heavy syrup. Allow the sugar syrup to cool before using. Most fruits will store well for 9–12 months in the freezer when packed in dry sugar or in a sugar syrup; this time is reduced to 3–6 months if frozen dry or as a purée.

Vegetables

It is necessary to blanch vegetables before freezing to stop enzyme action and to reduce micro organisms in the food which cause changes in the colour, texture and flavour. Freezing without blanching is possible but not normally recommended, as the freezer storage life is greatly reduced and much depends on the variety and quality of the vegetables at the time of freezing.

To blanch conventionally, the prepared vegetables are placed in a wire basket which is then plunged into a large pan containing $3\frac{1}{2}$l (6pt) boiling water for every 450g (1lb) vegetables. The blanching time is then calculated from when the water returns to the boil.

Blanching by microwave is much easier. The vegetables should be prepared for blanching in the normal way, placed in a large covered casserole dish with water, allowing 75–125ml (3–4fl oz) per 450g (1lb) vegetables. Heat for half the time given on the Vegetable Cooking Chart (page 12) when the vegetables will begin to change colour and become hot. It is important to shake or stir the vegetables at least once during the blanching time to ensure that they are evenly heated. After blanching, cool the vegetables in the normal way – in iced water – then drain, pack and freeze. Alternatively, for convenience, the vegetables may be blanched in boiling bags and then the whole package plunged up to the opening in iced water. This will chill the vegetables and expel the air in the bag at the same time, automatically creating a vacuum pack for the freezer. Seal the bag in the normal way and freeze.

In the same way as fruits, vegetables may also be 'open frozen' on trays for 1–2 hours before packing and sealing. The advantages of this method of freezing are that the fruits and vegetables do not become squashed during the freezing process and are easily separated when a small quantity is required from one pack. Most vegetables have a freezer storage life of 6–12 months; root vegetables, onions, leeks and cooked vegetable dishes for 2–6 months.

From the freezer

All frozen fruits and vegetables can be most successfully thawed and reheated or cooked in the microwave cooker. With most varieties no additional water is required, although this is a matter of personal preference and 2–3 × 15ml tbsp (2–3tbsp) water may be added. This applies to both home frozen produce as well as commercially frozen fruits and vegetables. If home frozen in cardboard cartons or boiling bags, fruits and vegetables may be cooked by microwave in their wrappings (but make sure to remove any metal or wire ties). This also applies to commercially frozen produce although some manufacturers use plastic bags which contain metal in the labelling on the packs and, therefore, the contents should be removed and placed in a suitable microwave container.

All frozen fruits and vegetables which are normally cooked in water should be covered to retain the moisture during cooking. Dishes with lids are best for larger quantities which require stirring during the cooking time as the lid may be removed easily. Clingfilm may be used to cover dishes or bowls but ensure that a slit is made with the pointed end of a sharp knife to prevent steam building up. Sealed, boilable pouches should also be slit or scored before placing in the microwave cooker.

During the defrosting and cooking period, gently shake or stir the contents of the cooking container to ensure even moisture distribution and heating. Solid packs of frozen fruits and vegetables should be broken down as soon as possible during the thawing and cooking time and the pieces of food separated. Season the cooking water or add salt very lightly during the first stirring when some of the liquid defrosted from the vegetables will help to dissolve it. Adjust seasoning if necessary at the end of the cooking time. Vegetable soups or fruit purées may be defrosted and reheated from the frozen state, breaking down the solid block as it begins to thaw for faster results. Ensure that the container is large enough to hold the food being thawed and to allow some room for stirring.

Frozen chips, which are normally fried, cannot be cooked in the microwave. Do not attempt to deep fat fry in the microwave as the temperature of the cooking fat or oil cannot be controlled. However, cooked chips can be reheated quite satisfactorily and commercially frozen oven chips are acceptable, although not crispy: 225g (8oz) oven chips should be cooked for 6–7 minutes spread over two thicknesses of kitchen paper towel during heating to absorb some of the moisture. Alternatively, they may be cooked in a browning dish which does give a more crispy result: preheat the browning dish for $3\frac{1}{2}$–4 min, place a single layer of chips on the bottom of the dish and cook for 5–6 min, turning the chips over once halfway through.

Fruit which has been frozen in dry sugar or sugar syrup may be defrosted on normal, full or high setting until the pieces can be separated. It is then better to allow the fruit to finish thawing at room temperature, particularly if it is important that the pieces remain whole. Dry-frozen fruits (free flow frozen) should be started off on a defrost or medium setting to commence thawing and then left to defrost completely at room temperature. Again, this is particularly important for soft fruits if they are wanted whole for serving. Frozen fruits which are to be cooked may be thawed and cooked from the frozen state in one operation – in the same way as frozen vegetables – but remember to stir or turn the dish during the heating period.

Cooked vegetable casseroles are best thawed using a defrost or medium setting, before heating through to ensure an even final result. This is particularly important if vegetables are coated in a sauce, otherwise the sauce may bubble and overheat before the vegetables are heated through.

Cooked fruit dishes, ie crumbles and tarts, should be thawed and reheated in a similar way, although if possible, cut fruit puddings into individual portions before heating through, when each portion will only take $\frac{1}{2}$–$1\frac{1}{2}$ min from frozen. If your microwave cooker does not have a defrost or medium setting, heat the frozen dish until warm to touch and then allow it to stand at room temperature until completely thawed before reheating. Alternatively, give the dish short 1–2 min bursts of microwave energy followed by resting periods and repeat until the food is thawed throughout.

Frozen fruit or vegetable pastry dishes, ie tarts, flans, quiches, should be either placed on, or covered with, kitchen paper towel to help in absorbing moisture from the food which otherwise would go back into the pastry during the defrosting and heating period.

Frozen fruit cooking chart

Fruit and quantity	30–50%
in dry sugar 450g (1lb)	4–8 min, stand until thawed
in sugar syrup 450g (1lb)	8–12 min stand until thawed
in dry pack (free flow or open frozen) 450g (1lb)	4–8 min, stand until thawed

Commercially frozen products may cook quicker than home frozen ones. This is due to the fact that commercial freezing takes place at very high speed and, as a result, the ice crystals are smaller and melt more quickly during cooking. The times given in the following charts are approximate, as the type and size of the container and the freezing method used will affect the cooking time required. Also the degree of cooking is a personal choice – some may prefer crispier vegetables whilst others prefer them cooked a little longer. Adjust the cooking times to suit your own individual requirements.

Frozen fruit and vegetable cooking charts
Fruit: Frozen fruits are partially defrosted by microwave and then allowed to stand at room temperature until completely thawed. Times are given in minutes for 450g (1lb) fruit. *Vegetables:* Frozen vegetables are defrosted and cooked in one operation.

Frozen vegetable cooking chart

Vegetable and quantity	Preparation	Cooking time on HIGH	Method
asparagus 225g (8oz) 450g (1lb)	arrange tips towards centre of the dish, cover	6–7 min 9–11 min	rearrange during cooking and stand 3–4 min
beans, broad 225g (8oz)	covered dish; add 2 × 15ml tbsp (2tbsp) salted water	7–8 min	stir during cooking and stand 3–4 min
beans, french 225g (8oz)	covered dish; add 3 × 15ml tbsp (3tbsp) salted water	6–7 min	stir during cooking and stand 2–3 min
beans, runner 225g (8oz)	covered dish; add 3 × 15ml tbsp (3tbsp) salted water	5–7 min	stir during cooking and stand 2–3 min
broccoli 225g (8oz) 450g (1lb)	covered shallow dish; add 4 × 15ml tbsp (4tbsp) salted water	6–7 min 9–11 min	stir during cooking and stand 3–4 min
cauliflower florets 225g (8oz) 450g (1lb)	covered dish; add 4–6 × 15ml tbsp (4–6tbsp) salted water	6–7 min 9–10 min	stir during cooking and stand 3–4 min
carrots 225g (8oz) 450g (1lb)	covered shallow dish; add 2–4 × 15ml tbsp (2–4tbsp) salted water	6–7 min 9–10 min	stir during cooking and stand 3 min
corn on the cob 2 cobs	wrap loosely in clingfilm or in buttered greaseproof paper	6–8 min	turn over during cooking and stand 2 min
courgettes 225g (8oz) 450g (1lb)	covered shallow dish	4–5 min 6–8 min	stir during cooking and stand 2–3 min
mixed vegetables 225g (8oz) 450g (1lb)	cook in pouch and slit the top	5–6 min 8–10 min	shake bag during cooking and stand 3–4 min
peas & sweetcorn 225g (8oz) 450g (1lb)	cook in slit pouch or in covered dish	4–5 min 7–8 min	shake pouch or stir and stand 2 min
spinach, chopped or leaf 225g (8oz)	covered shallow dish	6–7 min	break block and turn over during cooking
stewpack 225g (8oz)	covered shallow dish	6–7 min	stir during cooking and stand 2 min

on previous page:
Strawberry Ice Cream (page 113);
Strawberry Cream Flan (page 112)

From the storecupboard

Canned fruits and vegetables

Most canned foods are cooked during the processing and therefore only need reheating in the microwave. This applies to vegetables, fruits and canned pasta. The food must be removed from the can and placed in a suitable covered microwave container – on no account heat foods in the can.

Heat on normal, full or high setting for 3–4 min for the 400–425g (14–15oz) size and for 2–2½ min for the 200–225g (7–8oz) size. Stir the contents of the dish halfway through the cooking time to ensure even heating.

Pasta and rice

The main advantage of cooking pasta or rice by microwave is the fact that little or no attention is required during the cooking time and the kitchen remains relatively free of steam. When cooked, the results are excellent, with pasta just right at the *al dente* stage and rice grains just as they should be – separate, light and fluffy. There is no time saving over conventional methods as pasta and rice depend on the absorption of water to soften; therefore, once boiling, the cooking times are the same in all models of microwave cookers. Another plus feature, however, is that pasta and rice may be reheated most successfully; for best results either add a knob of butter or rinse under running water before heating.

When cooking pasta or rice, make sure the container is large enough to allow for the expansion of the food and that there is enough room for the water to boil. All dishes should be covered either with a lid or clingfilm during cooking.

Pasta and rice cooking chart

The times are given for 225g (8oz) pasta or rice on NORMAL, FULL OR HIGH setting, and from when the water has return to the boil.

Pasta/rice	Preparation	Cooking and standing time (in minutes)
egg noodles and tagliatelle	add 550ml (1pt) boiling salted water and 1 × 15ml tbsp (1tbsp) oil	5–6 + 3
macaroni	add 550ml (1pt) boiling salted water and 1 × 15ml tbsp (1tbsp) oil	8 + 3
pasta shells	add 850ml (1½pt) boiling salted water and 1 × 15ml tbsp (1tbsp) oil	15–18 + 2
spaghetti	break spaghetti in half if necessary; add 850ml (1½pt) boiling salted water and 1 × 15ml tbsp (1tbsp) oil	12 + 2
brown rice	add 550ml (1pt) boiling salted water	20–25 + 5
easy cook rice (american)	add 550ml (1pt) boiling salted water	12 + 5
long grain rice (patna)	add 550ml (1pt) boiling salted water and 1 × 15 ml tbsp (1tbsp) oil	10 + 5

Dried fruits and vegetables

Although dried fruits can be cooked without soaking, it is preferable to soak them overnight in cold water before cooking either conventionally or by microwave; this ensures plump and tender fruits. The exceptions are dates, figs, currants, sultanas, raisins etc, which do not require soaking before use in cake and pudding recipes unless specified. After soaking 225g (8oz) dried fruits for 6–8 hours or overnight, drain them and place in a suitable microwave container. Add about 275ml ($\frac{1}{2}$pt) boiling water, grated lemon rind or juice and sugar or syrup to taste and cook on normal, full or high setting for approximately 15 min, stirring or turning the dish once halfway through. Allow to stand for a few minutes before serving.

Dried peas, beans and lentils – pulses – require soaking before cooking conventionally or by microwave. They should be soaked in cold water for 8–12 hours, or overnight if possible. Alternatively, cover them with cold water and bring to the boil in the microwave, cook for 2–3 min then allow them to stand for 1–1$\frac{1}{2}$ hours to swell and soften. Drain and rinse well.

To cook, place the pulses in a large container, ensuring that there is sufficient room for the water to boil during cooking. Cover with boiling water from the kettle and bring the dish to the boil in the microwave cooker. Lentils take approximately 20–25 min to cook and larger pulses 40–60 min. All pulses should be covered during the cooking period. Be prepared to top up the cooking water with extra boiling water from the kettle when necessary.

Drying herbs

Preserving herbs by drying in the microwave is very quick and easy compared with conventional methods and the microwave cooker dries small quantities very successfully. Many varieties of herbs are annual plants and, when near the end of their season, it is possible to dry them by microwave to last through the winter months. The method is simple and the results are excellent, retaining better colours and aromas than conventionally dried herbs.

It is preferable if the herbs are clean and dry when picked, otherwise wash them thoroughly and pat them dry between pieces of kitchen paper towel. Gently squeeze as much moisture as possible from them after washing as this will help to cut down the drying time and give better results. Remove the leaves from the stems and measure about 1 cupful (25g/1oz). Spread out the herbs evenly onto two thicknesses of kitchen paper towel placed on the microwave cooker shelf and cover with two more pieces of kitchen paper towel. This helps to absorb moisture during the heating process.

Heat on 100% (full) setting for 4–6 min checking every min and turning the kitchen paper towel with the herbs over once. Check after minimum time – when dry, the herbs will be brittle and break very easily. Leave to cool between the kitchen paper towels before crushing and storing in an airtight jar which should be kept in a cool, dry place.

Preserves

There are many advantages in making chutneys, relishes, jams and marmalades in the microwave cooker. Apart from the fact that preserves can be made quickly with very little fuss or bother, the flavour is enhanced and, particularly important with jams and marmalades, a very good colour is retained. You will find that the kitchen remains free of smells and cooler too. It really is possible to make just one or two pots of jam or chutney without the worry of food burning or sticking onto the base of the cooking container.

Best results in fruit preserves are obtained with fresh fruits with a high pectin contect, ie citrus fruits, gooseberries and blackcurrants. Fruits low in pectin, ie strawberries and apricots, have citric acid, lemon juice or commercial pectin added. Jams, jellies and marmalades should be tested for setting point in the conventional way, by pouring a little onto a saucer and leaving it for a few minutes. If the skin formed on the top wrinkles when touched, setting point has been reached. Alternatively, a sugar thermometer can be used when the temperature should register 105°C (220°F), although some fruits may require a degree or two higher than this to obtain a better set. The sugar thermometer must not be left in the microwave when switched on, unless it has been specially designed for use in the microwave cooker. Use a 3½l (6pt) bowl or large dish for cooking your preserves, leaving enough room for expansion when they boil.

After cooking the preserve, the glass jars can be sterilised by pouring a little water into each and heating in the microwave until the water boils rapidly. Drain the jars and pour in the preserves. Top with waxed discs immediately and, when completely cold, cover with cellophane and label.

I have included a small selection of preserves in the recipe section and, using these as a guide, you will be able to adapt more of your own favourite recipes for cooking in the microwave.

Important notes

* All cooking is carried out in the microwave cooker using normal, full or high power unless otherwise stated. Some microwave cooking instructions are given for models with variable power control settings, but it is still possible to cook the dish on models without this facility by referring to the 'Variable Power Settings and Time Chart' on page 8 and calculating the time required for cooking on normal, full or high power. The automatic intermittent 'off' periods can be achieved manually by allowing the dish to rest at 1–2 min intervals throughout the cooking duration.

* The recommended cooking times are intended as a guide only, as so much depends on the power input to the microwave oven cavity, the shape, material and size of the dish, the temperature of the food at the commencement of cooking and the depth of food in the dish. If the quantities of food placed in the cooker are increased or decreased, then the cooking times must be adjusted accordingly. Always undercook rather than overcook the food, by cooking for a little less time than the recipe recommends, allowing the extra time if required.

* Microwave cooking does not brown food in the traditional way but dishes can be finished off in a conventional oven or under a grill if you feel it is necessary. For some dishes the alternative method of conventional cooking is given for those who prefer traditional browning.

* Metal baking tins or metal-trimmed dishes must not be used in the microwave cooker.

* Most fruit and vegetable dishes can be frozen successfully and therefore I have only noted those recipes in the book which require special attention for freezing, although obviously preserves do not need to be frozen.

A selection of preserves

Recipes

Apples

Apples are probably the most popular of all the fruits and can be divided into two groups – dessert or eating apples and cooking apples. Dessert apples are sweet and fragrant and are normally available all the year round as many varieties are imported. Cooking apples are nearly all home grown and are sharper in flavour. The flesh softens easily making them ideal for cooking, although some dessert apples, eg granny smiths, can be used equally well for either the table or for cooking.

Apple and cream cheese flan *(serves 6)*   *colour page 39*
POWER SETTING: NORMAL, FULL OR HIGH

1 20cm (8in) baked flan case (page 112)

For the filling:
3 medium dessert apples, peeled, cored and thinly sliced
½ lemon, juice and grated rind
sugar to taste
225g (8oz) cream cheese
50g (2oz) caster sugar
150ml (¼pt) double cream, whipped

For the glaze:
2 × 15ml tbsp (2tbsp) redcurrant jelly
1 × 15ml tbsp (1tbsp) lemon juice
2 × 15ml tsp (2tsp) water

For serving:
whipped cream

1 Place the apple slices in a large dish or on a plate. Sprinkle with the lemon juice and sugar to taste.
2 Cover with clingfilm and cook until just transparent, about 3–4 min. Drain the slices and leave to cool.
3 Cream the cheese and caster sugar together until soft, stir in the grated lemon rind and the whipped cream. Spread over the base of the flan case.
4 Place the redcurrant jelly, lemon juice and water in a bowl and heat for about 1 min until dissolved. Stir well and then boil in the microwave until thickened slightly – about 2–3 min, stirring frequently.
5 Arrange the apple slices over the cheese in the flan case and spoon the glaze over the apples.
6 Chill before serving with whipped cream.

Apple and raisin chutney *(makes about 1kg [2lb])*
POWER SETTING: NORMAL, FULL OR HIGH

450g (1lb) cooking apples, peeled, cored and sliced
1 large onion, chopped
1 clove garlic, finely chopped
25g (1oz) salt
225g (8oz) brown sugar
325ml (13fl oz) malt vinegar
225g (8oz) raisins
25g (1oz) ground ginger and dried mustard, mixed
½ × 5ml tsp (½tsp) cayenne pepper

This is a hot, spicy chutney, good for serving with cold meat or curries

1 Place the apples, onion, garlic, salt and sugar in a large bowl with the malt vinegar.
2 Cover and cook for approximately 10 min or until soft.
3 Purée the mixture in a blender or pass through a sieve. Add the raisins.
4 Mix the spices with a little of the purée and add to the chutney. Leave to stand overnight, then pot, seal and label.

Note: *If preferred, all the ingredients may be cooked together and potted without puréeing.*

Apple and rhubarb crumble *(serves 4–6)*
POWER SETTING: NORMAL, FULL OR HIGH

1 Lightly grease a 1¼l (2pt) pie dish or large soufflé dish.
2 Mix the prepared fruit and place in the bottom of the dish with the warmed golden syrup, lemon rind and juice.
3 Mix the flours with the salt and rub in the butter or margarine finely. Reserving a little of the demerara sugar and chopped walnuts, stir the remainder into the crumb mixture.
4 Sprinkle the crumb mixture lightly over the fruit and cook for 10–12 min, giving the dish a quarter turn every 3 min. Sprinkle the remaining demerara sugar and walnuts over the top of the crumble.
5 Serve hot or cold with custard or cream.

Alternative conventional bake
Cook in a preheated oven at 220°C (425°F) Mark 7 for about 45 min.

350g (12oz) cooking apples, peeled, cored and sliced
350g (12oz) rhubarb, washed, trimmed and cut into 2.5cm (1in) lengths
100g (4oz) golden syrup, warmed
1 lemon, grated rind and juice
175g (6oz) wholemeal and plain flour, mixed
pinch salt
75g (3oz) butter or margarine
50g (2oz) demerara sugar
2 × 15ml tbsp (2tbsp) chopped walnuts
For serving:
custard or cream

Apple jelly *(makes about 1kg [2lb])*
POWER SETTING: NORMAL, FULL OR HIGH

Windfall cooking apples may be used for this jelly but not dessert apples

1 Cut the apples into thick slices without peeling or coring. Place in a large bowl with the lemon juice and water.
2 Cover and cook for about 30–35 min until the apples are soft, stirring every 10 min.
3 Strain the pulp through a jelly cloth and measure the extract. There should be approximately 850ml (1½pt). (If it is more or less than this quantity, the sugar should be adjusted accordingly. You will need 450g (1lb) sugar for every 550ml (1pt) extract.)
4 Return the extract to the bowl and stir in the sugar until it has dissolved.
5 Cook uncovered for 30–35 min until setting point is reached, stirring every 10 min.
6 Pot, seal and label.

1.4kg (3lb) cooking apples, washed
1 lemon, juice
850ml (1½pt) water
675g (1½lb) preserving sugar, approximately

Note: *The jelly is a very pale colour – just tinged with pink. Add a few redcurrants or raspberries to the apples when cooking to give a slightly deeper colour if preferred.*

25

225g (8oz) cooking apples,
peeled, cored and thinly sliced

225g (8oz) damsons, washed
and stoned

50g (2oz) butter

100g (4oz) caster sugar

2 egg yolks

3 × 15ml tbsp (3tbsp) fresh
white breadcrumbs

150ml (¼pt) double cream

2 × 5ml tsp (2tsp) lemon
juice

For serving:
whipped cream

Apple and damson tansy *(serves 4)*
POWER SETTING: NORMAL FULL OR HIGH

Tansy is a bitter-tasting herb which was once used for flavouring sweet dishes. The name now describes a pudding made from buttered fruit purée with eggs; the recipe dates back to the fifteenth century

1 Place the prepared fruit in a covered dish or a roasting bag with the butter.
2 Cook for 6–8 min or until the fruit is soft, stirring or shaking the fruit once halfway through.
3 Pass the fruit through a sieve, or purée in a blender, and then sieve. The purée should be fairly thick. If it is too thin, allow to boil in the microwave for a minute or two until reduced slightly.
4 Stir the sugar into the hot purée until dissolved. Beat in the egg yolks and breadcrumbs and leave until cold.
5 Whisk the cream lightly and fold into the mixture with lemon juice to taste.
6 Place into individual serving glasses and chill in the refrigerator for an hour.
7 Serve piped with whipped cream.

THIS DISH IS NOT REALLY SUITABLE FOR FREEZING.

4 medium cooking apples

40g (1½oz) butter

50g (2oz) soft brown sugar

25g (1oz) sultanas

2 × 15ml tbsp (2tbsp)
chopped walnuts

2 × 15ml tbsp (2tbsp) water

1 × 15ml tbsp (1tbsp) lemon
juice

1½ × 15ml tbsp (1½tbsp) clear
honey

For serving:
cream

Honey baked apples *(serves 4)*
POWER SETTING: NORMAL, FULL OR HIGH

1 Core the apples but do not peel. Score them around the middle and place in a suitable serving dish.
2 Mix together the butter, sugar, sultanas and nuts. Fill the centre of each apple with the mixture.
3 Blend the water, lemon juice and honey together and spoon over the apples.
4 Cover the apples with lightly greased greaseproof paper and cook for 6–8 min.
5 Serve hot or cold with cream.

Note: *Cook 1 apple for 2–3 min; cook 2 apples for 4–5 min.*

450g (1lb) cooking apples,
washed

1 × 15ml tbsp (1tbsp) lemon
juice

6g (¼oz) root ginger

275ml (½pt) water

450g (1lb) preserving sugar

100g (4oz) preserved ginger,
finely chopped

Honey Baked Apples (above);
Apple and Damson Tansy (above)

Apple and ginger preserve *(makes about 675g [1½lb])*
POWER SETTING: NORMAL, FULL OR HIGH

1 Slice the apples without peeling and place in a large glass bowl with the lemon juice.
2 Bruise the ginger by hitting it with a rolling pin and add to the apples.
3 Add the water, cover with clingfilm and cook for 10 min. Remove the ginger.
4 Press the apples through a jelly cloth to extract all the juice. This should produce 550ml (1pt) of extract.
5 Add the sugar and preserved ginger to the extract. Stir until the sugar is dissolved. Cook uncovered for 25 min or until setting point is reached, stirring every 5 min.
6 Allow to cool for 20–30 min, stir then pot, seal and label.

Apricots

Apricots are small, stone fruit with golden, velvety skin and yellow, juicy flesh. Avoid any with soft and bruised brown skin. They are also excellent canned or dried.

Apricot and almond pudding (*serves 5–6*)   *colour page 118*
POWER SETTING: NORMAL, FULL OR HIGH

A pudding for a special winter lunch

100g (4oz) almonds, blanched
100g (4oz) shredded suet
100g (4oz) brown breadcrumbs
25g (1oz) wholemeal flour
5 × 15ml tbsp (5tbsp) apricot purée (page 29)
2 eggs, beaten
4–5 × 15ml tbsp (4–5tbsp) milk
For serving:
apricot purée and whipped cream

1 Lightly grease an 850ml (1½pt) pudding basin.
2 Reserve 8 almonds and chop the rest coarsely.
3 Place in a bowl and add the suet, breadcrumbs and wholemeal flour, mixing well together. Stir in the purée, eggs and milk.
4 Arrange the reserved almonds in the base of the prepared pudding basin and carefully spoon the mixture over the top. Smooth the surface.
5 Cover with clingfilm and slit with the pointed end of a sharp knife.
6 Cook for 7–8 min, turning once halfway through.
7 Leave to stand for 5 min before turning out.
8 Serve with hot apricot purée and whipped cream.

Note: *Apricot jam may be used instead of the apricot purée if preferred, although this will give a sweeter pudding.*

Apricot jam (*makes about 2¼kg [5lb]*)
POWER SETTING: NORMAL, FULL OR HIGH

1½kg (3½lb) apricots
225ml (8fl oz) water
6g (¼oz) citric acid
1¾kg (4lb) preserving sugar

1 Wash, halve and stone the apricots. Place in a large glass bowl with the water and citric acid.
2 Cover with a lid or clingfilm slit with the pointed end of a sharp knife. Cook for 15–20 min, stirring 2–3 times throughout.
3 Add the sugar and stir well. Cook uncovered for 45–50 min, or until setting point is reached, stirring every 5–10 min.
4 Allow to stand for 20–30 min. Warm the jars, then pot the jam, seal and label.

Apricot and date chutney (*makes about 1kg [2lb]*)
POWER SETTING: NORMAL, FULL OR HIGH

225g (8oz) apricots
225g (8oz) dates
50g (2oz) preserved ginger
100g (4oz) sultanas
100g (4oz) brown sugar
15g (½oz) salt
275ml (½pt) malt vinegar

1 Wash, halve and stone the apricots, stone the dates.
2 Roughly chop the apricots, dates and preserved ginger and place in a large bowl with the remaining ingredients.
3 Cover and bring to the boil in the microwave. Remove the cover, stir and cook for 20–30 min or until the desired consistency is reached, stirring every 5–10 min.
4 Allow to stand for 10 min, warm the jars then pot the chutney, seal and label.

Apricot purée *colour page 118*
POWER SETTING: NORMAL, FULL OR HIGH

450g (1lb) fresh apricots *or*
225g (8oz) dried apricots,
soaked overnight
1 lemon, grated rind
sugar to taste

1 Wash, stone and quarter the fresh apricots and place in a dish; cover and cook for 6–8 min until tender, stirring once throughout; or drain the dried apricots after soaking and place in a dish; add 550ml (1pt) boiling water. Cover and cook for about 15 min until tender, stirring once throughout. Drain.
2 Pass the fruit through a sieve, or alternatively purée in a blender and then pass through a sieve.
3 Add the grated lemon rind and sugar to taste.

Artichokes

Globe artichokes are imported mainly from countries around the Mediterranean. Choose young artichokes with close, fleshy scales, as it is the base of each leaf which is eaten by taking the flesh from the base with the teeth. The rest of the leaf is discarded, together with the fuzzy centre which is found when all the scales have been pulled. Below the leaves is the 'heart' of the artichoke which may be eaten and has the best flavour.

Jerusalem artichokes are knobbly tubers which can grow quite large; it is better to select good sized ones as there is less waste during preparation. They have a thin skin which may be peeled before cooking or rubbed off afterwards. The flesh is white and crisp and with a sweet flavour.

Chilled artichoke soup *(serves 6)*
POWER SETTING: NORMAL, FULL OR HIGH

450g (1lb) jerusalem artichokes, peeled
1 lemon, juice
50g (2oz) butter
1 onion, peeled and finely sliced
1 stick celery, finely sliced
700ml (1¼pt) boiling chicken stock
150ml (¼pt) dry white wine
bouquet garni
salt and freshly ground black pepper
150ml (¼pt) natural yoghurt
150ml (¼pt) double cream
For garnish:
chopped chives

1 Dice the artichokes and leave to soak for 5 min in a bowl of cold water with the lemon juice.
2 Drain the artichokes and pat dry.
3 Melt the butter in a large dish or bowl for 1½ min, add the artichokes, onion and celery; toss the vegetables well in the butter.
4 Cover and cook for 3–4 min. Add the boiling chicken stock, wine, bouquet garni and seasoning. Cover, bring to the boil in the microwave then continue cooking for 10–12 min, or until the vegetables are soft.
5 Remove bouquet garni and blend the soup in a liquidiser or pass through a sieve. Adjust the seasoning and leave to cool. Chill for 2–3 hours in the refrigerator.
6 Stir in the yoghurt and cream just before serving and sprinkle with chopped chives.

DO NOT FREEZE THE SOUP WITH THE YOGHURT AND CREAM – ADD THESE JUST BEFORE SERVING.

4 medium globe artichokes

150ml (¼pt) salted water

2 × 15ml tbsp (2tbsp) lemon juice

For the vinaigrette dressing:
150ml (¼pt) oil

3 × 15ml tbsp (3tbsp) wine vinegar

salt and freshly ground black pepper

1 × 15ml tbsp (1tbsp) chopped fresh herbs

Artichokes with vinaigrette dressing *(serves 4)*
POWER SETTING: NORMAL, FULL OR HIGH

An excellent starter when you have time to linger over a meal

1 Wash the artichokes and trim off the lower leaves if necessary.
2 Place in a large roasting bag or covered casserole dish with the salted water and lemon juice. Cook for 15–20 min, turning the dish or rearranging the artichokes twice throughout. Test if cooked by removing one of the leaves – it should pull away quite easily. Drain and leave to cool.
3 Blend the oil, vinegar and seasoning by whisking together in a bowl or placing in a screw top jar and shaking vigorously. Alternatively, blend in a liquidiser. Beat in the chopped herbs.
4 Serve the artichokes on individual dishes or plates, pour over a little dressing and hand the rest separately.

Note: *The artichokes may also be served hot with hollandaise sauce (page 33) or with melted butter.*

DO NOT FREEZE THE VINAIGRETTE DRESSING.

Asparagus

Although the season for home-grown asparagus is short – May, June and July – imported varieties are available from the beginning of the year. Asparagus is a member of the lily family and the two main types have either white fleshy stems with green tips or slender, green stems and tips. Avoid dirty, dry or woody stems and choose tips which are firm and tight.

450g (1lb) freshly cooked asparagus

For the mornay sauce:
25g (1oz) butter

25g (1oz) plain flour

275ml (½pt) milk

2 × 15ml tbsp (2tbsp) cooking water from the asparagus

2 × 15ml tbsp (2tbsp) cream

75–100g (3–4oz) cheddar cheese, grated

salt and freshly ground black pepper

paprika pepper for sprinkling

Asparagus in mornay sauce *(serves 4)*
POWER SETTING: NORMAL, FULL OR HIGH

This dish can be served as a starter, as part of a main course or as a light supper dish

1 Melt the butter in a large bowl for 1 min and stir in the flour until well blended.
2 Gradually add the milk mixed with the asparagus water, stirring continuously until smooth.
3 Heat for 3½–4½ min, whisking every 30 sec until the sauce is thickened and bubbling.
4 Stir in the cream, three-quarters of the cheese and season to taste.
5 Arrange the asparagus in the serving dish and reheat in the microwave if necessary. Pour over the sauce and sprinkle with the remaining cheese and a little paprika pepper.
6 Heat for 2–3 min in the microwave to melt the cheese, or brown under a hot grill.
7 Serve immediately.

FREEZE THE MORNAY SAUCE SEPARATELY.

Globe Artichokes with Hollandaise Sauce (above and page 33)

1 20cm (8in) baked flan case (page 112)

For the filling:

25g (1oz) butter or margarine

1 small onion, peeled and finely chopped

290g (10½oz) can condensed asparagus soup

3 eggs, beaten

3 × 15ml tbsp (3tbsp) single cream or top of the milk

salt and freshly ground black pepper

100g (4oz) cheese, finely grated

For garnish:

10–12 cooked asparagus spears, either fresh or frozen

Asparagus flan (*serves 6*)

POWER SETTING: NORMAL, FULL OR HIGH AND DEFROST OR MEDIUM

1 Melt the butter on normal, full or high setting for 1 min, toss in the chopped onion and cook for 2–3 min until soft.
2 Add the soup, eggs, cream and seasonings and pass the mixture through a sieve or purée in a blender.
3 Heat the mixture on defrost or medium setting for 6–8 min, whisking every 2 min. Stir in the cheese.
4 Pour the mixture into the flan case and cook on defrost or medium setting for 11–13 min, turning every 3 min. Allow to stand for 10–15 min.
5 If to be served hot, heat the cooked asparagus spears for 1–1½ min before arranging over the top of the flan.
6 Serve hot or cold as a snack, or with new potatoes and salad as a main course.

Alternative conventional bake

When the filling is added to the cooked flan case, cook in a preheated oven at 180°C (350°F) Mark 4 for 20–25 min until set and lightly brown. Heat the asparagus spears in the microwave as above and arrange over the top of the flan.

8 cooked pancakes (page 90)

For the filling:

350g (12oz) cooked asparagus, either fresh or frozen

275ml (½pt) mornay sauce (page 30)

For serving:

soured cream and chopped parsley

Asparagus pancakes (*serves 4 or 8*)

POWER SETTING: NORMAL, FULL OR HIGH

Almost any cooked vegetable can be used for this dish but asparagus is especially good

1 Roughly chop the asparagus, combine with the mornay sauce and, if necessary, heat the mixture for 2–3 min. Alternatively, if preferred, heat the asparagus spears and sauce separately.
2 Divide the sauce with the asparagus between the 8 pancakes, then fold over or roll up each one and place in a serving dish or on a plate.
3 Cover with a lid or clingfilm slit with the pointed end of a sharp knife and heat through for 2½–3½ min. Leave to stand for a few minutes.
4 Warm the soured cream for 15–30 sec. Uncover the pancakes and spoon the soured cream over the top.
5 Sprinkle with parsley and serve immediately.

DO NOT FREEZE THE PANCAKES WITH THE SOURED CREAM. FINISH AND GARNISH JUST BEFORE SERVING.

Asparagus with hollandaise sauce *(serves 4)*
POWER SETTING: NORMAL, FULL OR HIGH AND DEFROST OR MEDIUM

This delicious starter will complement almost any special lunch or dinner party

1 Trim and wash the asparagus spears. Place in a covered dish with the salted water and cook on normal, full or high setting for 11–12 min until tender, rearranging the spears halfway through. Leave to stand for a few minutes before draining and arranging on individual plates.
2 Melt the butter on defrost or medium setting for 2 min, add the vinegar and egg yolks and whisk lightly.
3 Cook on defrost or medium setting for 1 min, whisk well, season and serve immediately with the asparagus spears, handing the sauce separately.

Note: *Cooked asparagus may also be served cold with a vinaigrette dressing (page 30) or hot with melted butter.*

DO NOT FREEZE THE HOLLANDAISE SAUCE.

450g (1lb) medium asparagus spears
4 × 15ml tbsp (4tbsp) salted water
For the hollandaise sauce:
100g (4oz) butter
2 × 15ml tbsp (2tbsp) wine vinegar
2 egg yolks
salt and pepper

Aubergines (egg plants)

Aubergines, the fruit of the egg plant, are now available all the year round, imported from warm and sunny climates. Their shape varies from oblong to almost round and they weigh up to and sometimes over 450g (1lb). The skin is usually a deep purple but can also be green and near-white, whilst the flesh is a pale yellow-green. Aubergines can be sprinkled with salt and left to drain for about 30 min before cooking; this removes excess moisture and helps to tenderise them.

Aubergines au gratin *(serves 4)*
POWER SETTING: NORMAL, FULL OR HIGH AND DEFROST OR MEDIUM

1 Sprinkle the aubergine slices with salt and allow to stand for 30 min, then rinse well and dry.
2 Heat the oil in a large serving dish for 1 min, add the aubergine slices, toss well in the oil, cover and cook for 8–10 min until tender, stirring or shaking the dish twice throughout.
3 Add tomatoes, seasoning and herbs, cover and heat for about 2 min.
4 Beat the yoghurt with the eggs and stir in three-quarters of the cheese.
5 Wipe down the sides of the serving dish and pour the yoghurt topping over the aubergines.
6 Cook on defrost or medium setting for 9–10 min until the topping is set.
7 Sprinkle with the remaining cheese and cook on normal, full or high setting for 1–2 min until melted, or alternatively brown the top under a hot grill.
8 Serve straight away sprinkled with paprika pepper.

DO NOT FREEZE WITH THE TOPPING. FINISH AND GARNISH JUST BEFORE SERVING.

450g (1lb) aubergines, trimmed and finely sliced
salt
3 × 15ml tbsp (3tbsp) oil
200g (7oz) can tomatoes
salt and freshly ground black pepper
2 × 5ml tsp (2tsp) dried oregano or basil
275ml ($\frac{1}{2}$pt) natural yoghurt
2 eggs, beaten
100g (4oz) cheese, finely grated
paprika pepper for sprinkling

2 large aubergines

1 × 15ml tbsp (1tbsp) oil

1 onion, peeled and grated

2 × 15ml tbsp (2tbsp) natural yoghurt, approximately

1 × 5ml tsp (1tsp) cummin seeds, ground

2 × 15ml tbsp (2tbsp) lemon juice

1 green pepper, deseeded and chopped *or*

2 green chillies, chopped

salt to taste

For garnish:
onion rings

For serving:
lemon slices

Aubergine salad *(serves 6)*   *colour page 11*
POWER SETTING: NORMAL, FULL OR HIGH

This unusual salad is served as an accompaniment to curry

1 Wash the aubergines, prick the skins with a fork and brush over with the oil. Cover and cook in the microwave for 10–12 min until tender, turning the aubergines over once throughout.
2 Cut open the aubergines, scoop out the flesh and mash down with a fork.
3 Add onion, yoghurt, ground cummin and lemon juice. Mix well together and pass through a sieve, or purée in a blender. If the mixture is a little too thick, add some extra yoghurt or lemon juice.
4 Add the pepper or chillies and place the mixture in a serving dish.
5 Chill before serving, garnished with onion rings. Serve with lemon slices.

DO NOT FREEZE THIS DISH.

4 veal escalopes, about 100g (4oz) each

few drops of lemon juice

4 slices ham, about 25g (1oz) each

25g (1oz) butter

freshly ground black pepper

1 onion, peeled and thinly sliced

2–3 cloves garlic, crushed

450g (1lb) aubergines, trimmed and thinly sliced

4 tomatoes, skinned and quartered

1 × 15ml tbsp (1tbsp) tomato purée

salt

1 glass white wine or stock

50g (2oz) cheddar cheese, grated

For garnish:
chopped parsley

Veal with aubergine *(serves 4)*
POWER SETTING: NORMAL, FULL OR HIGH

1 Trim away any fat from the escalopes and beat into thin slices. Lay them out flat and sprinkle with a few drops of lemon juice.
2 Arrange a slice of ham on top of each escalope, then roll them up neatly and secure each one with cocktail sticks or tie with string.
3 Melt the butter in a large casserole for 1 min, arrange the veal rolls in the dish and turn or brush them with the butter. Sprinkle with black pepper.
4 Cover and cook for 8–10 min, turning the dish halfway through. Remove the veal rolls and keep warm.
5 Add the onion to the butter and juices in the dish, cover and cook for 2 min. Add the garlic and aubergines, toss over well, cover and cook for 6–8 min or until tender.
6 Add the tomatoes, tomato purée, salt to taste and the wine or stock. Cover and cook for 3–4 min.
7 Remove the cocktail sticks or ties from the veal and replace the rolls in the dish on top of the aubergine mixture; sprinkle with the grated cheese and reheat for 2–3 min until the cheese is melted.
8 Serve hot sprinkled with plenty of chopped parsley. Plain boiled potatoes in their jackets go well with this dish.

Baked Avocados with Walnut Cheese (page 37); Creamed Potatoes (page 102); Veal with Aubergine (above)

2 medium aubergines

salt

2 × 15ml tbsp (2tbsp) oil

2 medium onions, peeled and sliced

1 × 15ml tbsp (1tbsp) tomato purée

1 × 5ml tsp (1tsp) dried oregano or basil

200g (7oz) can tuna fish, drained

2 × 15ml tbsp (2tbsp) fresh brown breadcrumbs

2 × 15ml tbsp (2tbsp) grated parmesan cheese

2 × 15ml tbsp (2tbsp) grated gruyère cheese

4 × 5ml tsp (4tsp) melted butter

For serving:
green salad

Tuna-stuffed aubergines *(serves 2 or 4)*
POWER SETTING: NORMAL, FULL OR HIGH

1 Cut the aubergines in half lengthways, score the flesh with a knife, sprinkle with salt and allow to stand for 30 min. Rinse well and wipe dry.
2 Brush the cut surface with some of the oil, place cut side down on a plate, cover and cook for 8–10 min or until tender.
3 Heat the rest of the oil in a bowl for 1 min, add the onions, cover and cook for 5–6 min until soft. Add the tomato purée, herbs, tuna fish and breadcrumbs. Mix well together.
4 Scoop the flesh from the cooked aubergines and chop finely or mash down with a fork. Add to the bowl with the tuna fish mixture and heat through for 1–2 min.
5 Pile the mixture into the aubergine skins, sprinkle with the mixed grated cheeses and add 1 × 5ml tsp (1tsp) butter to each aubergine half.
6 Heat through for 4–5 min until the cheese is melted. Alternatively, brown the top under a hot grill.
7 Serve hot or cold with a green salad.

Avocado pears

The avocado pear resembles a vegetable rather than a fruit with its soft texture and delicate, nutty flavour. The skin is a dark green, almost purple colour, whilst the rich, oily flesh is much paler and when ripe and ready to eat is a soft yellow-green.

Avoid fruits with soft dark indentations on the skin. Ripe avocados will yield to a little pressure on the skin but if purchased when firm, they will ripen within a few days in a warm room.

1 large avocado pear, ripe

1 lemon, grated rind and juice

75g (3oz) cream cheese

salt and freshly ground black pepper

150ml (¼pt) soured cream

25g (1oz) gelatine

150ml (¼pt) water

few drops green food colouring, optional

For serving:
mixed salad

Avocado ring mould *(serves 4–6)*   *colour page 7*
POWER SETTING: NORMAL, FULL OR HIGH

Serve as a starter to a meal or as part of a summer buffet party

1 Halve and stone the avocado. Scoop out the flesh with a spoon into a large bowl.
2 Add the lemon rind and juice and mash down with a wooden spoon. Add the cream cheese and seasoning and blend well together. If preferred, purée in a blender or pass through a sieve. Add the soured cream.
3 Sprinkle the gelatin over the water in a bowl and heat in the microwave for 15–30 sec until the gelatin is dissolved.
4 Pour in a stream onto the avocado mixture, stirring continuously, until blended together. Add a few drops of green food colouring.
5 Pour into a ring mould and chill for several hours in the refrigerator before serving.
6 Turn out of mould before serving with mixed salad.

DO NOT FREEZE THIS DISH.

Baked avocados with walnut cheese *(serves 4)*   *colour page 35*
POWER SETTING: NORMAL, FULL OR HIGH

2 avocado pears, ripe
few drops of lemon juice
50g (2oz) butter
100g (4oz) cream cheese
50g (2oz) walnuts
freshly ground black pepper
For serving:
lemon wedges

This is an unusual way of serving avocado pears as a starter and makes a change from the normal 'vinaigrette' or 'with prawns'

1 Cut the avocados in half, remove the stones and sprinkle each half with a little lemon juice.
2 Place the avocado halves in a microwave dish with the narrow ends towards the centre. Cover with a lid or clingfilm slit with the pointed end of a sharp knife.
3 Place in the microwave and cook for 5–7 min until soft, depending on the ripeness of the pears. Allow to stand for a few minutes. (The avocado flesh will slightly darken during the cooking.)
4 Meanwhile, cream the butter and cheese together until light. Reserving 4 walnut halves, chop the remainder very finely and mix into the creamed butter and cheese. Add freshly ground black pepper to taste.
5 Uncover the avocados and divide the walnut and cheese mixture between the 4 halves. Heat for 1 min – just enough time to warm the topping.
6 Add a walnut half to each avocado and serve hot with lemon wedges.

DO NOT FREEZE THIS DISH.

Bananas

Bananas are normally imported whilst green, stored and then sold as they ripen. Avoid any squashy fruits when buying; the yellow skins should be just flecked with brown – not with black patches. It is normally preferable to choose from a 'hand' of bananas than to buy them loose. The firmer green bananas are better for cooking as they slice more easily. Bananas will keep for up to a week in a cool place; do not store in a refrigerator as the skins will turn black.

Banana custard pie *(serves 6)*
POWER SETTING: NORMAL, FULL OR HIGH

1 20cm (8in) baked flan case
(page 112)
For the filling:
15g (½oz) cornflour
15g (½oz) caster sugar
275ml (½pt) milk
1 egg, beaten
vanilla essence
1 × 15ml tbsp (1tbsp)
raspberry jam
2 bananas, peeled and sliced
For decoration:
banana slices, glacé cherries
and angelica

The old favourite 'bananas and custard' is made into something a little more special with this recipe

1 Mix the cornflour with the sugar and blend with a little of the milk. Gradually add the rest of the milk.
2 Cook for 3–4 min until thick, stirring every minute.
3 Whisk the custard well to cool it slightly before adding the egg and vanilla essence. Continue to whisk until the custard is smooth and creamy.
4 Spread the raspberry jam over the base of the flan case and then layer the custard and banana slices alternately ending with a layer of custard.
5 Decorate with banana slices (sprinkled with a little lemon juice to stop them discolouring) and tiny pieces of cherry and angelica.

DO NOT FREEZE THIS DISH.

4 firm bananas

few drops lemon juice

50g (2oz) butter

40–50g (1½–2oz) demerara sugar

2–3 × 15ml tbsp (2–3tbsp) brandy, rum or orange liqueur

Bananas flambé (serves 4)
POWER SETTING: NORMAL, FULL OR HIGH

1 Peel the bananas and cut in half lengthways, sprinkle with lemon juice.
2 Melt the butter in a serving dish for 1–2 min, add the demerara sugar and heat for 1 min.
3 Add the bananas and spoon over some of the butter and sugar. Cover and cook for 4–5 min.
4 Heat brandy, rum or liqueur in an ovenproof glass for 15–30 sec or until hot.
5 Remove cover from bananas, ignite the brandy, rum or liqueur and pour over the bananas. Do not ignite in the microwave.
6 Serve immediately and spoon the juices over the bananas.

DO NOT FREEZE THIS DISH.

6 large, firm bananas

1 apple, peeled, cored and grated

2 × 15ml tbsp (2tbsp) lemon juice

25g (1oz) butter

1 large onion, peeled and finely sliced

1 clove garlic, finely chopped

1–2 × 5ml tsp (1–2tsp) curry powder

1 × 5ml tsp (1tsp) turmeric

2 sticks celery, thickly sliced

150ml (¼pt) mayonnaise

150ml (¼pt) natural yoghurt

salt to taste

For serving:

plainly boiled rice and desiccated coconut

Banana salad (serves 6–8)   colour page 11
POWER SETTING: NORMAL, FULL OR HIGH

This unusual salad is flavoured with curry powder and may be served as a main course or as part of a buffet menu

1 Peel and slice the bananas and mix with the grated apple. Sprinkle with the lemon juice.
2 Melt the butter for 1 min in a large bowl, add the onion and garlic. Cover and cook for 2–3 min.
3 Add the curry powder and turmeric, stir well, cover and cook for 2 min.
4 Stir in the bananas, apple and celery, cover and cook for 4 min until heated through and to combine the flavours. Leave to cool.
5 Mix the mayonnaise with the yoghurt, stir into the cold banana mixture and add salt to taste.
6 Pile into the centre of a bed of cooked, cold rice and serve chilled, sprinkled with desiccated coconut.

Note: *Chopped, cooked chicken may be added to the dish, in which case a little more mayonnaise or yoghurt will be needed to blend the mixture.*

DO NOT FREEZE THIS DISH.

Beans

Broad Beans have thick pods which become furry inside when mature. At this stage, the beans are shelled before cooking, but when very young and freshly picked both pods and beans are edible and make an excellent vegetable.
French Beans vary from being mid-green with plump, round pods to pale green with flatter pods. They are usually stringless when young and can be cooked whole or cut through into 2.5–3.75cm (1–1½in) lengths.
Runner Beans are larger and coarser than french beans, although usually they have more flavour. Except when very young, they require stringing before slicing thinly and cooking.
Dried Beans are the dried seeds of leguminous plants. When served as a vegetable allow 50–75g (2–3oz) per person (dried weight) and leave to soak before cooking (page 21) or soak and use them as specified in the recipes.

Bananas Flambé (above); Peaches with Raspberry Purée (page 93); Apple and Cream Cheese Flan (page 24)

For the bèchamel sauce:
1 small onion, peeled
6 cloves
1 bay leaf
6 peppercorns
1 blade mace
275ml (½pt) milk
25g (1oz) butter
25g (1oz) flour
salt and pepper

450g (1lb) shelled broad beans
2 × 15ml tbsp (2tbsp) salted water
2 × 15ml tbsp (2tbsp) cream
225g (8oz) lean ham, shredded
1 × 15ml tbsp (1tbsp) freshly chopped parsley

Broad beans with ham *(serves 4–6)*
POWER SETTING: DEFROST OR MEDIUM AND NORMAL, FULL OR HIGH

1 To make the sauce, stick the onion with the cloves and place in a bowl with the rest of the spices and the milk. Heat without boiling on defrost or medium setting for 10 min. Leave to stand for 10–20 min to allow the infusion of the flavours from the spices into the milk. Strain the milk. Melt the butter for 1 min, stir in the flour, salt and pepper and add the milk a little at a time until well blended, stirring continuously. Cook for 1½–2 min, stirring every 30 sec until thickened and bubbling. Adjust the seasoning if necessary.
2 Cook the broad beans with the salted water in a suitable covered container for 8–10 min. After cooking, if the beans are old, remove the thin skins.
3 Add the beans to the sauce with the cream and ham. Cook for 2–3 min until heated through.
4 Stir in the chopped parsley and serve.

Note: *225–350g (8–12oz) butter beans, soaked and cooked (page 21), can be used instead of broad beans for this dish.*

450g (1lb) french beans, trimmed and left whole
2 × 15ml tbsp (2tbsp) salted water
6 × 15ml tbsp (6tbsp) olive oil
2 × 15ml tbsp (2tbsp) lemon juice or wine vinegar
salt and freshly ground black pepper
pinch sugar
For garnish:
1 hardboiled egg

French bean salad *(serves 4–6)*
POWER SETTING: NORMAL, FULL OR HIGH

French beans, lightly cooked and served cold, make an excellent ingredient for a mixed salad, or can be served on their own with a plain dressing

1 Wash the beans and place with the salted water in a serving dish. Cover and cook for 6 min, shaking or stirring the beans twice throughout. Leave to stand for a few minutes. The beans should be crisp.
2 Whisk the olive oil, lemon juice or wine vinegar, seasoning and sugar together.
3 Drain the beans, add the dressing and allow to cool.
4 When cold, toss the beans in the dressing.
5 Separate the egg white from the yolk. Chop the white finely and rub the yolk through a sieve.
6 Garnish the beans attractively with the egg yolk and white and serve.

DO NOT FREEZE THIS DISH.

Mixed bean salad 1 *(serves 4–6)*

Follow the recipe for french bean salad (above), but add some cooked or canned red kidney beans and cooked haricot beans to the dish before garnishing with the egg.

DO NOT FREEZE THIS DISH.

Green Beans Italian Style (page 42); Broad Beans with Ham (above); French Bean Salad (above)

Mixed bean salad 2 (*serves 4–6*)

Arrange an assortment of soaked and cooked or canned pulses on a serving platter, using about 100–175g (4–6oz) each of red kidney beans, haricot beans, butter beans etc. Choose the variety to suit what is available. Pour over an oil and vinegar dressing, ie vinaigrette (page 30) or french (page 44), with a little chopped garlic added. Garnish with a few chopped capers or freshly chopped herbs and serve with raw shredded spinach.

DO NOT FREEZE THIS DISH.

Green beans Italian style (*serves 4*)   colour page 41
POWER SETTING: NORMAL, FULL OR HIGH

450g (1lb) runner or french beans, prepared and sliced thickly

2 × 15ml tbsp (2tbsp) salted water

40g (1½oz) butter

1–2 × 15ml tbsp (1–2tbsp) olive oil

2 × 5ml tsp (2tsp) freshly chopped parsley or sage

1–2 cloves garlic, crushed

salt and freshly ground black pepper

2–3 × 5ml tsp (2–3tsp) grated parmesan cheese

For garnish:
freshly chopped herbs

Runner or french beans can be used for this dish – a good way of serving beans towards the end of their season

1 Wash the beans and place with the salted water into a serving dish, cover and cook for 8–10 min. Allow to stand for a few minutes.
2 Melt the butter for 1½ min, add the olive oil, parsley or sage and garlic and heat for 1 min.
3 Add the drained beans, salt and pepper to taste, toss well, cover and cook for 3 min. Stir in the parmesan cheese to taste.
4 Serve hot garnished with chopped herbs.

Note: *225g (8oz) can tomatoes may be added with the beans before adding the parmesan cheese. Allow an extra 1½ min cooking time.*

Cassoulet (*serves 4–6*)   colour page 87
POWER SETTING: NORMAL, FULL OR HIGH OR DEFROST OR MEDIUM

225g (8oz) haricot beans, soaked

boiling water

1 small onion, peeled and finely chopped

4–5 cloves garlic

2 × 5ml tsp (2tsp) salt

225g (8oz) streaky pork, cut into small pieces

175g (6oz) lean lamb or mutton, cut into small pieces

2 × 5ml tsp (2tsp) french mustard

ground black pepper

425g (15oz) can tomatoes

3–4 × 15ml tbsp (3–4tbsp) tomato purée

275ml (½pt) boiling chicken stock, approximately

bouquet garni

225g (8oz) garlic or smoked sausage

browned breadcrumbs

Cassoulet is a French dish from the region of Languedoc. There are several local variations of the recipe but nearly all include lamb or goose with pork or bacon and garlic or smoked sausage. Haricot beans are the principal ingredient and this recipe is strongly flavoured with tomatoes and garlic. Normally the dish is cooked very slowly for anything up to 5 hours, but this microwave version is cooked much more quickly. Flavours will infuse and improve if the dish is allowed to cool, then placed in a refrigerator overnight and reheated the next day. It is a rather substantial dish and excellent for a cold winter's day

1 After the haricot beans have been soaked (page 21), drain and rinse. Pour on boiling water from the kettle to cover the beans. Allow to stand for 5 min, then drain and place the beans in a 2l (3½pt) dish.
2 Add the onion, garlic and salt, pork, lamb, mustard, pepper, tomatoes and tomato purée. Mix well together then pour on half the boiling chicken stock. Stir well and add the bouquet garni.
3 Cover and cook for EITHER 1 hour on normal, full or high setting OR 2 hours on defrost or medium; stir 2–3 times throughout and add more boiling stock as and when necessary. At the end of the cooking time the mixture should be fairly thick as the liquids are absorbed.
4 Add the garlic or smoked sausage and continue cooking for 15 min on normal, full or high setting OR 20–30 min on defrost or medium. At the end of the cooking time, the beans should be tender. Remove bouquet garni.

5 If to be served the same day, sprinkle the top of the dish with browned breadcrumbs and cook for 4–5 min on normal, full or high setting OR 8–10 min on defrost or medium. Allow to stand for 15 min before serving.

6 If to be served the next day, allow to cool and refrigerate overnight. Before serving, heat for 8–10 min on normal, full or high setting, stirring 2–3 times throughout. Sprinkle with the browned breadcrumbs and heat for 4–5 min. Allow to stand for a few minutes before serving.

Note: *The choice of power settings and cooking times are dependent upon the time you have available.*

Beetroot

Beetroot can be cooked so quickly in the microwave that the problem of them bleeding during the conventional long, slow cooking time is almost completely dispelled. If buying beetroot already cooked, look for fresh skins which are slightly moist; those with dry shrivelled skins can be woody and tough.

Although it is perhaps more common to serve beetroots with a salad, they really are delicious when hot – as a vegetable in their own right.

Beetroot American style *(serves 4–6)*
POWER SETTING: NORMAL, FULL OR HIGH

This recipe uses small, whole beetroot, but it is possible to use large beetroot cut into slices

1 Peel the beetroots and keep whole. If using larger beetroots, cut into thick slices.
2 Melt the butter for 1 min, add the garlic and cook for 1 min.
3 Stir in the flour. Make up the lemon juice or wine vinegar to 275ml (½pt) with water.
4 Add the liquid to the butter and flour mixture gradually, stirring all the time and add the sugar and seasonings. Cook for 4–5 min until thickened and bubbling, stirring every 30 sec.
5 Adjust seasonings, adding a little more sugar or lemon juice/wine vinegar if necessary. The sauce should taste sharp and sweet.
6 Chop one of the baby beetroots (or use 2 slices) very finely and stir into the sauce. Add the rest of the beetroots and cook for 1–2 min or until heated through.
7 Serve hot, sprinkled with parsley.

450g (1lb) cooked baby beetroots
25g (1oz) butter
1 clove garlic, crushed
25g (1oz) flour
2 × 15ml tbsp (2tbsp) lemon juice or wine vinegar
1 × 15ml tbsp (1tbsp) sugar
1 × 5ml tsp (1tsp) salt
freshly ground black pepper
For garnish:
freshly chopped parsley

1 onion, peeled and finely chopped

1 large carrot, peeled and finely chopped

2–3 sprigs parsley

1 bay leaf

salt and freshly ground black pepper

1l (1¾pt) boiling chicken stock

450g (1lb) cooked beetroot, chopped

150ml (¼pt) soured cream

For garnish:

chopped chives or mint

Borsch *(serves 4–6)*   *colour page 49*
POWER SETTING: NORMAL, FULL OR HIGH

This beetroot soup can be served hot or cold, with soured cream swirled over the top to give a good colour contrast

1 Place the onion, carrot, herbs, seasoning and boiling stock into a large serving dish. Cover and cook for 5 min.
2 Add the beetroot and cook for 10 min. Remove bay leaf.
3 Purée the soup in a blender, then strain through a sieve into the serving dish.
4 Wipe the edges of the dish, stir in the soured cream and serve hot. If serving cold, chill in the refrigerator and stir in the cream just before serving.
5 Serve sprinkled with chopped chives or mint.

DO NOT FREEZE WITH THE SOURED CREAM. FINISH AND GARNISH JUST BEFORE SERVING.

2 large beetroots, weighing 225g (8oz) each

1 large cooking apple

1 medium onion, peeled and grated or finely chopped

4 × 15ml tbsp (4tbsp) french dressing

½ clove garlic, crushed

chopped parsley

Beetroot salad *(serves 4–6)*
POWER SETTING: NORMAL, FULL OR HIGH

1 Scrub the beetroots, prick the skin once or twice with a fork and wrap in clingfilm.
2 Cook for 18–20 min in the microwave cooker. Test whether cooked with a skewer or knife. Allow to stand for 5 min.
3 Peel the beetroots, cut into dice and allow to cool.
4 Peel, core and cut the apple into dice, stir in the chopped onion.
5 Beat the dressing and garlic together.
6 Mix the beetroot with the apple and onion and add the dressing.
7 Sprinkle with chopped parsley and serve.

Note: *A little grated horseradish may be added for a really sharp-flavoured salad.*

French dressing

Whisk 1 × 15ml tbsp (1tbsp) wine vinegar with ½ × 5ml tsp (½tsp) salt and freshly ground black pepper. Add 3 × 15ml tbsp (3tbsp) salad oil and whisk or beat well. Alternatively, place in a screw top jar and shake vigorously or blend in a liquidiser.

DO NOT FREEZE THIS DISH.

Cherries with Claret (page 58); Blackcurrant Brulée (page 46)

2 large beetroots, weighing about 225g (8oz) each
1 × 15ml tbsp (1tbsp) salad oil
salt and pepper
150ml (¼pt) soured cream
chopped chives

Beetroot in soured cream *(serves 4–6)*   *colour page 7*
POWER SETTING: NORMAL, FULL OR HIGH

An alternative way to serve a beetroot salad

1 Cook the beetroots the same way as for beetroot salad (page 44) and allow to stand for 5 min.
2 Peel the beetroots and slice thinly. Allow to cool.
3 Brush the beetroot with a little salad oil and then arrange in overlapping slices in the serving dish.
4 Beat the soured cream with a fork and pour over the beetroot slices. Sprinkle with chopped chives.

Note: *The beetroot may also be served hot with soured cream. After cooking, peel, slice and brush with a little melted butter or oil. Arrange in the serving dish and keep warm. Heat the soured cream for 15–30 sec and pour over the beetroot slices. Sprinkle with chopped chives.*

DO NOT FREEZE THIS DISH.

Blackcurrants

These are normally sold stripped from their stalks. Their season is very short and they are not always available as most are bought for commercial use. For these recipes, frozen blackcurrants may be used if fresh ones are not in season.

450g (1lb) blackcurrants, stalks removed
75–100g (3–4oz) brown sugar
3 × 5ml tsp (3tsp) arrowroot
2 × 15ml tbsp (2tbsp) white rum
275ml (½pt) soured cream
demerara sugar and ground cinnamon for sprinkling

Blackcurrant brulée *(serves 6)*   *colour page 45*
POWER SETTING: NORMAL, FULL OR HIGH

1 Wash the blackcurrants and place in a bowl, cover and cook for 2 min. Stir or shake gently, add the brown sugar and mix well together. Cover and cook for 3 min.
2 Blend the arrowroot with the white rum, add to the blackcurrants, mix well and heat for 1–2 min or until thickened. Pour into a heatproof serving dish or individual dishes and leave to cool.
3 When cold, pour the soured cream over the top of the blackcurrants and sprinkle with the demerara sugar mixed with a pinch of cinnamon to taste.
4 Brown the top under a hot grill until the sugar bubbles and caramelises.
5 Chill before serving.

Note: *Blackberries or raspberries may also be used for this dish. If soured cream is not available, a mixture of half double cream and half natural yoghurt makes a good substitute.*

DO NOT FREEZE WITH THE SOURED CREAM. ADD THE TOPPING AND FINISH UNDER A HOT GRILL JUST BEFORE SERVING.

Blackcurrant jam *(makes about 1kg [2lb])*
POWER SETTING: NORMAL, FULL OR HIGH

450g (1lb) blackcurrants
425ml (¾pt) boiling water
675g (1½lb) preserving sugar

1 Remove stalks, wash the fruit, drain well and place in a large bowl with the boiling water.
2 Bring to the boil in the microwave then cook for about 5 min until the fruit is tender.
3 Stir in the sugar until dissolved.
4 Cook uncovered for 25–30 min or until setting point is reached, stirring every 5 min.
5 Allow to stand for 20 min and then pour into warmed jars. Seal and label.

Broccoli

Broccoli is related to the cabbage and cauliflower family and is gradually becoming more popular. The green or deep purple 'heads' should be close and firm. If they are beginning to open or flower, it is an indication that the broccoli will be tough and without flavour.

Broccoli in butter sauce *(serves 4)*
POWER SETTING: NORMAL, FULL OR HIGH

450g (1lb) green broccoli, washed and trimmed
4 × 15ml tbsp (4tbsp) salted water
For the sauce:
50g (2oz) butter
2 × 5ml tsp (2tsp) plain flour
1 egg yolk
juice of half a lemon
2 × 15ml tbsp (2tbsp) double cream
salt and pepper

The green broccoli, or calabrese, contrasts well with the creamy white sauce. Serve as a starter or as a special vegetable dish with the main course.

1 Place the broccoli in a casserole dish with the salted water. Cover and cook for 8–12 min. (Cooking time will vary with the size of the broccoli heads.) Allow to stand for a few minutes, then drain and reserve the cooking liquor. Keep warm.
2 Melt the butter for 1–2 min, stir in the flour and blend well together. Stir in the broccoli cooking liquid. Heat for 2–3 min until thickened.
3 Beat the egg yolk with the lemon juice and some of the hot sauce. Blend well together and add to the sauce, beating well.
4 Stir in the cream and heat for 15–30 sec, but do not allow sauce to boil. Adjust seasoning.
5 Pour the sauce over the broccoli in the dish and serve immediately.

DO NOT FREEZE THIS DISH.

450g (1lb) broccoli spears, washed and trimmed

2 × 15ml tbsp (2tbsp) salted water

For the sauce:

25g (1oz) butter

25g (1oz) flour

salt and pepper

275ml (½pt) chicken stock

3 × 15ml tbsp (3tbsp) double cream

2 × 5ml tsp (2tsp) french mustard

few drops of lemon juice

3 × 15ml tbsp (3tbsp) browned breadcrumbs

3 × 15ml tbsp (3tbsp) grated cheese

Broccoli au gratin *(serves 4)*
POWER SETTING: NORMAL, FULL OR HIGH

Broccoli should be undercooked to preserve its delicate flavour. It may be served as an accompaniment to a main meal but also makes an excellent first course served with hollandaise sauce (page 33) or au gratin

1 Place the prepared broccoli spears in a roasting bag, boiling bag or covered casserole dish, add the salted water and cook for 8–12 min. (Cooking time will vary with the thickness of the spears.) Allow to stand for a few minutes.
2 Melt the butter for 1 min, add the flour and seasoning, stir well until blended, then gradually add the stock, stirring well after each addition.
3 Heat for 3–4 min until thickened, whisking every 30 sec. Allow to cool slightly then beat in the cream, mustard and lemon juice.
4 Drain the broccoli spears and arrange in a serving dish or individual dishes. Spoon the sauce over the broccoli.
5 Mix the browned breadcrumbs and cheese together and sprinkle over the sauce. Heat for 2 min until the cheese has melted, or brown under a hot grill.
6 Serve hot.

FREEZE THE SAUCE SEPARATELY.

Brussels sprouts

Brussels sprouts, the popular winter vegetable available from early autumn through the winter, are improved by frost. Choose tightly closed sprouts and avoid any with loose, dropping leaves which show signs of yellowing. Too often, sprouts are overcooked – to their detriment. They should be cooked until just crisp, and served piping hot, when they are delicious.

50–75g (2–3oz) butter

1 clove garlic, finely chopped

5–6 × 15ml tbsp (5–6tbsp) toasted breadcrumbs

450g (1lb) brussels sprouts, cooked

salt and freshly ground black pepper

few drops of lemon juice

Brussels sprouts with buttered breadcrumbs *(serves 4)*
POWER SETTING: NORMAL, FULL OR HIGH

A good way of using up any left-over sprouts – quickly reheated by microwave

1 Melt the butter in a serving dish for 1–2 min, add the garlic, breadcrumbs and seasoning.
2 Toss well, then add the brussels sprouts. Cook uncovered for 2½–3½ min, stirring once halfway through.
3 Serve hot, sprinkled with lemon juice to taste.

Note: *If preferred, the ingredients may be cooked in a browning dish which has been preheated for 4–5 min; toss over well so that the breadcrumbs become golden brown.*

Brussels Sprouts with Buttered Breadcrumbs (above); Borsch (page 44); Broccoli au Gratin (above)

450g (1lb) chestnuts
50g (2oz) butter
2 × 15ml tbsp (2tbsp)
chicken stock
675g (1½lb) brussels sprouts,
trimmed and washed
3 × 15ml tbsp (3tbsp) salted
water
salt and freshly ground black
pepper

Brussels sprouts with chestnuts *(serves 6–8)*
POWER SETTING: NORMAL, FULL OR HIGH

An excellent vegetable dish to serve with poultry or game

1 Skin the chestnuts by slitting the skins with a sharp knife and then heating 10 or 12 at a time in the microwave until hot, 1–1½ min. Peel off the skins while hot.
2 Cook the chestnuts in half the butter and stock in a covered dish until soft, 10–12 min. Leave to stand for a few minutes.
3 Cook the sprouts in a suitable container or roasting or boiling bag with the salted water for 11–13 min. Drain the sprouts and the chestnuts.
4 Melt the remaining butter for 1 min, add the drained sprouts and chestnuts and mix well together.
5 Serve hot.

450g (1lb) brussels sprouts,
freshly cooked
150ml (¼pt) soured cream
1 × 5ml tsp (1tsp) freshly
grated nutmeg

Brussels sprouts with soured cream *(serves 4)*
POWER SETTING: NORMAL, FULL OR HIGH

An unusual dressing for a popular winter vegetable

1 Place the sprouts in a serving dish and if necessary reheat for 2–3 min.
2 Beat the soured cream with the nutmeg and pour over the sprouts. Toss well and heat for 15–30 sec.
3 Serve immediately.

DO NOT FREEZE THIS DISH.

Cabbages

There are many different types of cabbage, round or oval in shape and blue-green, green, white or red in colour, with loose or tightly packed leaves. It is probably one of the most popular vegetables but should not be over-cooked as so often is the case. Correctly served, plain cabbage can be delicious when cooked by microwave.

Chinese cabbage. This vegetable is becoming more popular and makes a delicious change from the usual varieties. It can be used in salads but may also be cooked like ordinary cabbage – either shredded or in quarters. Chinese cabbage requires very little water so reduce the water quantity to 1 × 15ml tbsp (1tbsp) when cooking as a plain vegetable, but try using it instead of white cabbage for the recipes in this section.

Creamed cabbage *(serves 4)*
POWER SETTING: NORMAL, FULL OR HIGH

40g (1½oz) butter
1 small onion, peeled and
finely chopped
1 × 15ml tbsp (1tbsp) flour
salt and pepper
150ml (¼pt) single cream or
top of the milk
450g (1lb) shredded cabbage,
freshly cooked and drained
grated nutmeg for sprinkling

1 Melt the butter in a serving dish for 1–1½ min. Add the onion, toss well, cover and cook for 3 min.
2 Stir in the flour and seasoning and blend together. Gradually add the single cream or milk.
3 Cook for 2–3 min until thickened. Stir in the freshly cooked cabbage and heat through for 2–3 min.
4 Serve hot sprinkled with grated nutmeg.

Braised white cabbage *(serves 6)*
POWER SETTING: NORMAL, FULL OR HIGH

1 medium firm white cabbage
25g (1oz) butter
1 large onion, peeled and
sliced
1 cooking apple, peeled and
sliced
salt and pepper
2 × 15ml tbsp (2tbsp) stock

1 Cut the cabbage into quarters, cut away the core and shred the leaves finely. If you are using the hard, white Dutch cabbage, cook with 3 × 15ml tbsp (3tbsp) salted water for 4 min. Drain. This is not necessary for green cabbage.
2 Melt the butter in a large dish for 1 min, add the onion, cover and cook for 2 min. Add the apple, cover and cook for 2 min.
3 Stir in the cabbage, seasoning and stock. Cover and cook for 15–20 min until tender.
4 Serve hot.

German red cabbage *(serves 4–6)*
POWER SETTING: NORMAL, FULL OR HIGH

450g (1lb) red cabbage, very
finely shredded
50g (2oz) butter, melted
1 large onion, peeled and
sliced
2 cloves garlic, finely chopped
1 cooking apple, peeled and
sliced
1 bay leaf
pinch each of dried parsley
and thyme
pinch each of ground
cinnamon and nutmeg
salt and freshly ground black
pepper
1 orange, grated rind
2 × 15ml tbsp (2tbsp) brown
sugar
1 × 5ml tsp (1tsp) caraway
seeds
1 small wine glass red wine

1 Toss the shredded cabbage in the melted butter, cover and cook for 3–4 min.
2 Add all the other ingredients and stir well. Cover and cook for 20–25 min, stirring 2–3 times throughout.
3 Remove bay leaf and serve hot.

8 large cabbage leaves, trimmed and washed

2 × 15ml tbsp (2tbsp) salted water

25g (1oz) butter

1 large onion, peeled and finely chopped

350g (12oz) cooked chicken or ham, minced

1 × 15ml tbsp (1tbsp) chopped parsley

4 × 15ml tbsp (4tbsp) fresh white breadcrumbs

200–225g (7–8oz) can tomatoes

salt and freshly ground black pepper

For serving:

tomato sauce (page 114)

Stuffed cabbage leaves *(serves 4)*

POWER SETTING: NORMAL, FULL OR HIGH AND DEFROST OR MEDIUM

This is a good way of using up left-over cold meats and makes a substantial main course

1 Place the cabbage leaves with the salted water in a boiling or roasting bag and cook for 4–5 min. Drain well.
2 Melt the butter for 1 min, add the onion, toss well, cover and cook for 5–6 min until transparent and soft.
3 Stir in the minced cooked chicken or ham, parsley and breadcrumbs.
4 Drain the tomatoes and reserve the juice. Add the tomatoes to the meat mixture with sufficient of the juice to moisten. Add salt and pepper to taste.
5 Divide the mixture between the cabbage leaves, then roll up each one into a parcel and secure with a cocktail stick or tie with string.
6 Place the cabbage leaves into a buttered serving dish, cover and cook on defrost or medium setting for 8–10 min until heated through.
7 Serve hot with tomato sauce.

Carrots

Carrots – nourishing and inexpensive – are available all the year round. Young carrots are often purchased in bunches with the green tops still intact. After removing these, the tender carrots only require washing before use. Larger, older carrots require either scraping or peeling before cooking. Carrots should be firm and crisp when buying, avoid any which are limp or pitted.

Carrot and cucumber vichy *(serves 6–8)*

POWER SETTING: NORMAL, FULL OR HIGH

1 Follow the ingredients and recipe for glazed carrots (page 54).
2 Peel a cucumber, cut in half lengthways and cut each half in 1.25cm ($\frac{1}{2}$in) slices.
3 Cook the cucumber in a covered casserole dish or roasting bag or boiling bag for 3–4 min until tender. Drain the cucumber and add to the glazed carrots with the parsley, making sure that all the vegetables are coated in the glaze.

DO NOT FREEZE THIS DISH.

Greek Lemon Soup (page 74); Stuffed Cabbage Leaves (above)

225g (8oz) new carrots, washed

2 × 15ml tbsp (2tbsp) salted water

15g ($\frac{1}{2}$oz) butter

1 × 5ml tsp (1tsp) caster sugar

225g (8oz) frozen peas

sprig of mint

freshly ground black pepper

Carrots flamande (serves 4)
POWER SETTING: NORMAL, FULL OR HIGH

1 Leave the carrots whole if small, otherwise cut them in halves or quarters.
2 Place the carrots in a casserole dish with the salted water, butter and sugar. Cover with a tight-fitting lid or clingfilm.
3 Cook for 6–7 min until the carrots are tender, stirring 3 times throughout. Add the peas, mint and freshly ground black pepper.
4 Stir well to mix the vegetables, cover and cook for a further 4–5 min.
5 Remove the lid or clingfilm and continue to cook until the water has evaporated, about 1$\frac{1}{2}$–2 min.
6 Remove the mint, adjust seasoning and serve.

450g (1lb) carrots, washed or peeled

4 × 15ml tbsp (4tbsp) salted water

25g (1oz) butter

freshly ground black pepper

1 × 5ml tsp (1tsp) caster sugar

1 × 15ml tbsp (1tbsp) chopped parsley

Glazed carrots (serves 4)   colour page 15
POWER SETTING: NORMAL, FULL OR HIGH

1 If the carrots are young, cut into quarters or leave whole; if the carrots are large, cut into thin slices.
2 Place the carrots in a casserole dish with the salted water, butter, pepper and sugar.
3 Cover with a tightly fitting lid or clingfilm and cook for 9–10 min until tender, shaking or stirring 3 times throughout.
4 Remove the lid or clingfilm and cook for 1–2 min until the water has evaporated leaving the butter and sugar glaze around the carrots. Stir frequently.
5 Stir in the chopped parsley and serve hot.

Glazed carrots with orange

Follow the recipe and method for glazed carrots, replacing the salted water with orange juice, the caster sugar with brown sugar and stirring in the finely grated rind of an orange instead of the parsley.

Cauliflower

The cauliflower is produced for its undeveloped flower rather than the leaves. When buying, ensure that the leaves are green and crisp and the head is white and tightly packed. Avoid any with brown, grey or damaged curds.

1 cauliflower about 675g (1$\frac{1}{2}$lb)

4 × 15ml tbsp (4tbsp) salted water

40g (1$\frac{1}{2}$oz) butter

50g (2oz) flaked almonds, toasted

4 × 15ml tbsp (4tbsp) fresh brown breadcrumbs

Cauliflower almondine (serves 4–6)
POWER SETTING: NORMAL, FULL OR HIGH

1 Trim the cauliflower and wash. Place in a large casserole dish with the salted water. Cover and cook for 10–11 min. Leave to stand for 5 min.
2 Melt the butter for 1$\frac{1}{2}$ min. Add the almonds and breadcrumbs, toss over well so that the breadcrumbs are evenly coated with the butter.
3 Cook uncovered for 3–4 min.
4 Drain the cauliflower and place in its dish. Spoon or sprinkle over the almond and breadcrumb mixture.
5 Serve hot.

DO NOT FREEZE THIS DISH.

Cauliflower with mushrooms *(serves 4–6)*
POWER SETTING: NORMAL, FULL OR HIGH

1 Place the cauliflower florets and salted water into a boiling or roasting bag and cook for 10–11 min, shaking or turning every 2 min. Leave to stand for a few minutes.
2 Melt the butter for 1 min, add the mushrooms and cook for 2 min.
3 Stir in the flour and seasoning and blend well together. Add the milk gradually then cook for 5–6 min until the sauce is thickened and bubbling. Stir every 30 sec.
4 Drain the cauliflower and place in its serving dish. Stir the cream into the sauce and heat for 15 sec.
5 Pour the sauce over the cauliflower and serve immediately garnished with sprigs of parsley.

FREEZE THE SAUCE SEPARATELY.

1 large cauliflower, cut into florets
4 × 15ml tbsp (4tbsp) salted water
25g (1oz) butter
175g (6oz) button mushrooms, washed
25g (1oz) flour
salt and freshly ground black pepper
275ml ($\frac{1}{2}$pt) milk
2 × 15ml tbsp (2tbsp) single cream
For garnish:
parsley sprigs

Cauliflower with vegetable sauce *(serves 4–6)*   *colour page 57*
POWER SETTING: NORMAL, FULL OR HIGH

This is a very quick and easy but different way of serving cauliflower using canned vegetable oil pâté (available from health food shops) as the base for the sauce

1 Trim and wash the cauliflower. Place in a large casserole dish with the salted water. Cover and cook for 10–11 min.
2 Drain the cauliflower well after cooking and keep warm in a serving dish.
3 Blend the vegetable oil pâté with the single cream and cook for 2–3 min until hot, do not allow to boil.
4 Pour the sauce over the cauliflower and serve hot sprinkled with freshly chopped parsley.

DO NOT FREEZE THIS DISH.

1 cauliflower, about 675g ($1\frac{1}{2}$lb)
4 × 15ml tbsp (4tbsp) salted water
1 small can or tube vegetable oil pâté
150ml ($\frac{1}{4}$pt) single cream
For garnish:
freshly chopped parsley

Celeriac

From the celery family, celeriac is an edible root which is becoming more popular. The roots vary in size and have a fibrous brown skin. The white flesh has a delicate celery flavour and a crisp texture.

Celeriac salad *(serves 4)*   *colour page 7*
POWER SETTING: NORMAL, FULL OR HIGH

1 Cut the peeled celeriac into julienne strips or matchstick-size pieces. Place in a dish with the salted water. Cover and cook for 3–4 min, tossing every minute, until the celeriac is just blanched.
2 Drain and rinse under cold running water.
3 Beat the mayonnaise and cream together and toss the celeriac in the dressing.
4 Sprinkle with the chives or parsley and serve chilled with slices of salami, ham or smoked salmon.

DO NOT FREEZE THIS DISH.

1 celeriac, peeled
3 × 15ml tbsp (3tbsp) salted water
2 × 15ml tbsp (2tbsp) mayonnaise
2 × 15ml tbsp (2tbsp) soured cream
1 × 5ml tsp (1tsp) chopped chives or parsley

Celery

Although celery is most often served in salads or used as a flavouring in soups and stews, it also makes a good vegetable dish. It can vary in colour from white to pale green. Firm heads with crisp leaves are an indication of freshness.

1 large head celery

150ml (¼pt) boiling chicken stock

4 × 15ml tbsp (4tbsp) browned breadcrumbs

100g (4oz) cheddar cheese, grated

slivers of butter

paprika pepper for sprinkling

Celery au gratin (serves 4)
POWER SETTING: NORMAL, FULL OR HIGH

1 Trim the celery and cut into 4 lengthways. Remove the leaves and wash the celery.
2 Place the celery quarters in a shallow dish with the chicken stock, cover and cook for 12–15 min until tender. Drain off the stock.
3 Mix the browned breadcrumbs and grated cheese together and sprinkle over the celery.
4 Dot with slivers of butter and cook uncovered for 3–4 min until the cheese and butter are melted.
5 Sprinkle with paprika pepper and serve hot.

1 onion, peeled and chopped

½ head celery, trimmed and roughly chopped

225g (8oz) frozen peas

550ml (1pt) boiling chicken stock

salt and pepper

1 bay leaf

bouquet garni

1 × 15ml tbsp (1tbsp) cornflour

150ml (¼pt) milk

150ml (¼pt) single cream

For garnish:
freshly chopped parsley

Celery and pea soup (serves 4–6)
POWER SETTING: NORMAL, FULL OR HIGH

1 Place the onion, celery, peas and stock into a large casserole dish or bowl. Add salt and pepper, bay leaf and bouquet garni.
2 Cover and cook for 12–15 min until the vegetables are tender.
3 Remove bay leaf and bouquet garni. Blend the soup in a liquidiser or pass through a sieve.
4 Blend the cornflour with the milk and then add to the soup in the bowl. Heat for 3–4 min or until slightly thickened and boiling.
5 Stir in the cream to give a swirled effect and serve sprinkled with chopped parsley.

DO NOT FREEZE WITH THE CREAM. FINISH AND GARNISH JUST BEFORE SERVING.

Cherries

Cherries are related to the plum family, and come in many different varieties. Dessert cherries are sweet and vary in colour from white or pink to almost black. Morello cherries are more acid in flavour and are best for cooking or for jam making.

Celery and Pea Soup (above); Cauliflower with Vegetable Sauce (page 55)

425–450g (15–16oz) can black cherries
1 × 15ml tbsp (1tbsp) sugar
2 × 5ml tsp (2tsp) arrowroot, blended with a little cold water
4 × 15ml tbsp (4tbsp) brandy or cherry brandy
For serving:
vanilla ice cream

Cherries jubilee *(serves 4)*
POWER SETTING: NORMAL, FULL OR HIGH

1 Drain the cherries and reserve the juice. Remove the stones from the cherries.
2 Place the juice and the sugar in a bowl or jug and add the arrowroot blended with a little cold water.
3 Cook for 3–4 min until thickened and bubbling, stirring every 30 sec.
4 Add the cherries to the sauce and cook for 1–2 min until heated through. Remove from the microwave.
5 Heat the liqueur for 15–30 sec until hot, pour over the cherries and ignite. Do not ignite in the microwave.
6 Spoon the cherries and sauce over scoops of vanilla ice cream and serve quickly.

DO NOT FREEZE THIS DISH.

675g (1½lb) cherries with stalks removed
1 bottle claret
sugar to taste
pinch cinnamon
3 × 15ml tbsp (3tbsp) redcurrant jelly
For serving:
sponge fingers

Cherries with claret *(serves 6)*   colour page 45
POWER SETTING: NORMAL, FULL OR HIGH AND DEFROST OR MEDIUM

1 Wash the cherries, drain and dry.
2 Place the claret in a large serving dish, cover and bring to the boil on normal, full or high setting in the microwave about 8–10 min.
3 Add the cherries, sugar and cinnamon and simmer in the microwave on defrost or medium setting for 8–10 min until the cherries are tender.
4 Remove the cherries from the dish with a slotted spoon. Bring the wine up to the boil in the microwave on normal, full or high setting and cook until the liquid is reduced by one-third.
5 Stir in the redcurrant jelly until dissolved. Add the cherries to the syrup and allow to cool.
6 Serve cold with sponge fingers.

Note: *Frozen or drained, canned cherries may be used for this dish, in which case they do not require cooking in the wine syrup.*

Chicory

Chicory is normally used as a salad vegetable. Choose heads which are firm with tightly packed leaves and avoid any which are yellowing or wilting. Chicory may also be served as a cooked vegetable, requiring very little additional water whether cooked conventionally or by microwave.

4 heads of chicory, trimmed
25g (1oz) butter, melted
1 × 15ml tbsp (1tbsp) salted water
1 × 15ml tbsp (1tbsp) lemon juice
freshly ground black pepper

Braised chicory *(serves 4)*
POWER SETTING: NORMAL, FULL OR HIGH

1 Cut the heads of chicory in half lengthways and place in a casserole dish with the butter, salted water and lemon juice.
2 Cover with a tightly fitting lid or clingfilm and cook 6–7 min, shaking the dish 2–3 times throughout.
3 Adjust seasoning and sprinkle with freshly ground black pepper.

DO NOT FREEZE THIS DISH.

Chicory in ham sauce *(serves 4)*
POWER SETTING: NORMAL, FULL OR HIGH

1 Cut the heads of chicory in half lengthways and place in a casserole dish with the water and lemon juice.
2 Cover with a lid or clingfilm and cook for 6–7 min until tender, shaking or turning the dish 2–3 times throughout. Leave to stand for a few minutes.
3 Melt the butter in a bowl, stir in the flour and seasoning and blend together. Stir in the mustard.
4 Add the milk gradually and cook for 3–4 min until thickened and bubbling, stirring every 30 sec. Stir in three-quarters of the cheese and beat well. Stir in the ham.
5 Drain the chicory and coat with the sauce. Sprinkle with the remaining cheese and paprika pepper. Top with the slivers of butter.
6 Cook for 2–3 min until the cheese is melted and bubbling, or alternatively brown under a hot grill.

THE SAUCE ONLY MAY BE FROZEN. FINISH AND TOP WITH THE BUTTER JUST BEFORE SERVING.

4 heads chicory, trimmed
1 × 15ml tbsp (1tbsp) water
1 × 15ml tbsp (1tbsp) lemon juice
For the sauce:
15g (½oz) butter
15g (½oz) flour
salt and pepper
½ × 5ml tsp (½tsp) french mustard
275ml (½pt) milk
50g (2oz) gruyère cheese, grated
50g (2oz) lean ham, cut into strips
paprika pepper for sprinkling
few slivers of butter

Corn on the cob/sweetcorn

Corn on the cob should have stiff, green leaves or husks when fresh and the grains should be soft, milky and shiny. The tassels should be removed before cooking. The husks too, are normally removed before cooking conventionally, but in the microwave they may be left on and removed before serving. Do not season before cooking conventionally or in the microwave, as salt tends to toughen the grains.

Frozen and canned cobs and sweetcorn kernels are obtainable all the year round and make a good accompaniment, or base, for a variety of dishes.

Cream of chicken and sweetcorn soup *(serves 4)*
POWER SETTING: NORMAL, FULL OR HIGH

1 Heat the oil in a large bowl for 1–2 min, add the onion and celery, cover and cook for 3 min.
2 Add the chicken stock, sweetcorn and seasonings and cook for 5 min. Add the chicken and cook for 2 min.
3 Blend the soup with the milk in a liquidiser or pass through a sieve. Reheat the soup for 2 min.
4 Stir in the cream and serve sprinkled with the flaked almonds.

Note: *If preferred, the soup may be served without puréeing. Use 550ml (1pt) boiling chicken stock and omit the milk. Thicken the soup with 2 × 5ml tsp (2tsp) arrowroot mixed with a little water, then stir in the cream or top of the milk. Mix the almonds into the soup before serving.*

DO NOT FREEZE WITH THE CREAM. FINISH AND GARNISH JUST BEFORE SERVING.

1 × 15ml tbsp (1tbsp) oil
1 onion, peeled and finely chopped
1 stick celery, chopped
425ml (¾pt) boiling chicken stock
225g (8oz) sweetcorn kernels, fresh or frozen
salt and pepper
100g (4oz) cooked chicken, diced
150ml (¼pt) milk
3 × 15ml tbsp (3tbsp) single cream or top of the milk
25g (1oz) flaked almonds, toasted

1 × 5ml tsp (1tsp) turmeric *or* a few strands of saffron

225ml (8fl oz) distilled malt vinegar

1 red pepper, deseeded and diced

1 green pepper, deseeded and diced

1 stick celery, finely chopped

1 onion, peeled and finely chopped

1 clove garlic, finely chopped

675g (1½lb) sweetcorn kernels, fresh, frozen or canned

225g (8oz) caster sugar

pinch each of mustard, mace, tarragon

2 × 15ml tbsp (2tbsp) arrowroot, blended with a little water

Sweetcorn relish *(makes about 1½kg [3lb])*
POWER SETTING: NORMAL, FULL OR HIGH

1 Add the turmeric or saffron to the vinegar and leave to turn yellow whilst preparing the vegetables.
2 Strain the vinegar into a large bowl and add the vegetables except the sweetcorn. Cover and cook for 5 min.
3 Add the sweetcorn, sugar and seasonings. Stir well and cook for 5 min.
4 Add the arrowroot blended with water to the mixture. Stir well and cook for 5 min, stir, then cook for 3 min or until thickened.
5 Leave to cool slightly then pot, seal and label.

1 20cm (8in) baked flan case (page 112)

For the filling:

25g (1oz) butter or margarine

1 small onion, peeled and finely chopped

75ml (2½fl oz) milk

200g (7oz) can sweetcorn

200g (7oz) can tuna fish, drained and flaked

2 eggs, beaten

salt and freshly ground black pepper

75g (3oz) cheese, finely grated

Sweetcorn and tuna flan *(serves 6)*   *colour page 7*
POWER SETTING: NORMAL, FULL OR HIGH AND DEFROST OR MEDIUM

1 Melt the butter or margarine in a large bowl for 1 min, add the onion, toss well, cover and cook for 3 min until soft.
2 Add the milk and contents of the can of sweetcorn with the tuna fish. Beat in the eggs and the seasoning. Stir in half the cheese.
3 Pour into the flan case and sprinkle with the remaining cheese.
4 Cook on defrost or medium setting for 14–16 min, turning every 3 min. Leave to stand for 10–15 min.
5 Serve hot or cold with salad.

Alternative conventional bake
It is not necessary to bake the pastry case first. Cook the complete dish in a preheated oven at 190°C (375°F) Mark 5 for 40–50 min.

Courgettes

Courgettes (or zucchini) are baby marrows specially grown and picked. They can vary in size up to about 15cm (6in) long but should be straight and firm. Depending on their size, they may be cooked whole or in slices.

Courgette Flan (page 62)

225g (8oz) courgettes

225g (8oz) tomatoes, skinned

1 small onion, peeled and finely chopped

1 clove garlic, crushed

1 × 15ml tbsp (1tbsp) vinegar

salt and freshly ground black pepper

1 × 15ml tbsp (1tbsp) chopped parsley

50g (2oz) cheese, finely grated

Casserole of courgettes (serves 4)
POWER SETTING: NORMAL, FULL OR HIGH

1 Wash and trim the courgettes and cut into thin slices. Slice the tomatoes.
2 Place in a covered dish with the onion, garlic, vinegar and seasoning. Cook for 12–14 min.
3 Stir in the parsley and sprinkle with the grated cheese. Cook for 2–3 min until the cheese is melted, or brown under a conventional hot grill.

1 20cm (8in) baked flan case (page 112)

For the filling:

25g (1oz) butter or margarine

1 onion, peeled and finely sliced

1 × 15ml tbsp (1tbsp) olive oil

225g (8oz) courgettes, trimmed and finely sliced

2 cloves garlic, crushed

2 eggs, beaten

150ml (¼pt) natural yoghurt or milk

2 × 5ml tsp (2tsp) dried oregano or basil

2 × 15ml tbsp (2tbsp) tomato purée

salt and freshly ground black pepper

For serving:

crusty french bread

Courgette flan (serves 6)   colour page 61
POWER SETTING: NORMAL, FULL OR HIGH AND DEFROST OR MEDIUM

1 Melt the butter or margarine for 1 min in a large bowl, add the onion, mix well together and cook for 2 min.
2 Add the oil, sliced courgettes and garlic, toss well together, cover and cook for 5–6 min until the vegetables are soft, turning or shaking twice throughout.
3 Beat the eggs with the yoghurt or milk, add the herbs, tomato purée and seasonings. Add this to the onions and courgettes and heat on defrost or medium setting for 3–4 min until hot, stirring every minute.
4 Pour into the flan case and cook on defrost or medium setting for 10–12 min until set. Allow to stand for 10–15 min.
5 Serve hot or cold with crusty french bread.

Alternative conventional bake
When the filling is added to the flan case, cook in a preheated oven at 180°C (350°F) Mark 4 for 20–25 min until set.

Courgettes maison *(serves 4 or 8)*   *colour page 118*
POWER SETTING: NORMAL, FULL OR HIGH OR DEFROST OR MEDIUM

1 Place the courgettes in a large dish, cover and cook for 4–5 min. Rinse in cold water.
2 Cutting lengthways, remove and discard a thin strip from the top of each courgette. Scoop out the flesh from each courgette and chop finely.
3 Melt the butter in a bowl for 1 min. Add the onion, cover and cook for 2 min.
4 Remove the seeds from the tomatoes, chop the flesh and add to the onions with the flesh from the courgettes, paprika pepper and seasonings. Cover and cook for 3 min.
5 Stir the prawns with the mixture and divide between the courgette cases.
6 Cover the dish and cook for a further 3–4 min.
7 Mix the bèchamel sauce with half the cheese and spoon over the courgettes. Sprinkle the remaining cheese and paprika pepper over the top of the sauce.
8 Cook, uncovered, for 2–3 min on normal, full or high setting or for 5 min on defrost or medium.
9 Allow 1 courgette per person if serving as a starter course, or 2 per person if serving as a main dish.

FREEZE THE SAUCE SEPARATELY. FINISH AND GARNISH JUST BEFORE SERVING.

8 small courgettes, trimmed and washed
25g (1oz) butter
1 onion, finely chopped
4 tomatoes, skinned
1 × 5ml tsp (1tsp) paprika pepper
salt and freshly ground black pepper
225g (8oz) shelled prawns
275ml (½pt) bèchamel sauce (page 40)
50g (2oz) grated parmesan cheese
paprika pepper for sprinkling

Cranberries

These small fruits have a slightly bitter flavour. They can vary in colour from pale pink to dark red and are normally used for sauces and preserves. If freshly picked, they will require topping and tailing before use.

Cranberry sauce *(makes about 275ml [½pt])*
POWER SETTING: NORMAL, FULL OR HIGH

1 Place the cranberries in a covered dish, roasting bag or boiling bag with the sugar and water.
2 Cook for 5–6 min or until fruit is soft.
3 Add the butter, stir until melted then cook, uncovered, for 1 min.
4 Serve hot or cold with roast turkey or chicken.

450g (1lb) cranberries, washed
100g (4oz) sugar
1 × 15ml tbsp (1tbsp) water
25g (1oz) butter

Spiced cranberry preserve *(makes about 275ml [½pt])*
POWER SETTING: NORMAL, FULL OR HIGH

1 Place the cranberries in a covered dish with the spices and cider vinegar.
2 Cook for 5–6 min or until the fruit is soft.
3 Add the demerara sugar and cook for a further 3 min.
4 Remove root ginger, cinnamon stick and cloves.
5 Pot and seal in small jars.
6 Serve cold with roast turkey or chicken.

225g (8oz) cranberries, washed
small piece each of root ginger and cinnamon stick
6 cloves
½ × 5ml tsp (½tsp) ground allspice
150ml (¼pt) cider vinegar
100g (4oz) demerara sugar

Cucumbers

Cucumbers, although available all the year round, are at their best in late summer. Choose firm, crisp, straight cucumbers with a slight bloom on the skin. Although they are normally associated with salads, try serving them hot, as a vegetable in their own right. When cooked in the microwave they retain their full flavour and crisp texture.

1 large cucumber, washed
40g (1½oz) butter
100g (4oz) button mushrooms, washed
1 × 5ml tsp (1tsp) cornflour
75ml (2½fl oz) chicken stock
75ml (2½fl oz) single cream
few drops soy sauce
100g (4oz) shelled prawns
For garnish:
freshly chopped chives or dill
lemon or cucumber twists

Chinese cucumber starter *(serves 4)*
POWER SETTING: NORMAL, FULL OR HIGH

1 Cut the cucumber into 1.25cm (½in) dice, place in a dish, cover and cook for 3 min. Drain.
2 Melt the butter in a bowl for 1–1½min, add the mushrooms, cover and cook for 2 min. Add the cucumber and cook for 3 min until the vegetables are tender but crisp.
3 Blend the cornflour with the stock, add the cream and soy sauce. Pour over the vegetables and heat for 1–2 min. Stir in the prawns and continue to heat for 1–2 min.
4 Divide the mixture between 4 individual serving dishes and garnish with the chopped herbs and lemon or cucumber twists.
5 Serve hot.

Note: *Tiny, button mushrooms are best but if the mushrooms are large, cut into slices before cooking.*

DO NOT FREEZE THIS DISH.

25g (1oz) butter or margarine
1 onion, peeled and sliced
850ml (1½pt) boiling chicken stock
1 large cucumber, peeled and roughly chopped
1 sprig of mint
salt and pepper
2 × 5ml tsp (2tsp) cornflour
150ml (¼pt) double, single or soured cream
a few drops green food colouring, optional
For garnish:
diced cucumber or chopped mint

Cream of cucumber soup *(serves 4–6)*
POWER SETTING: NORMAL, FULL OR HIGH

1 Melt the butter or margarine in a large bowl for 1 min, add the onion and toss well in the butter. Cover and cook for 2 min.
2 Add the stock, cucumber, mint and seasoning. Cover and cook for 30 min. Remove the mint.
3 Purée the soup in a blender or pass through a sieve.
4 Blend the cornflour with a little of the soup, then add it to the rest and cook for 3–4 min until it thickens.
5 Adjust the seasoning and stir in the cream. Add a few drops of green colouring if necessary.
6 Serve hot or very cold garnished with cucumber or chopped mint.

Chinese Cucumber Starter (above);
Fennel Sauce (page 67)

Dates

Fresh dates are plump with brown, shiny skins. The pulpy flesh is sugary and sweet. Dried dates are similar in appearance but avoid any with sugar crystals; they are also available stoned which is perhaps more convenient for cooking purposes.

450g (1lb) dates, roughly chopped
450g (1lb) raisins
1 medium onion, peeled and finely chopped
350g (12oz) brown sugar
2 cloves garlic, crushed
2 × 5ml tsp (2tsp) salt
4–6 chillies, finely chopped
550ml (1pt) vinegar

Date chutney (makes about 1¼kg [2½lb])
POWER SETTING: NORMAL, FULL OR HIGH

1 Place all ingredients in a large bowl and cover with a lid, or clingfilm slit with the pointed end of a sharp knife.
2 Bring the mixture to the boil and cook until tender and the desired consistency is reached, about 30 min.
3 Leave to cool slightly then pot, seal and label.

100g (4oz) dates, roughly chopped
150ml (¼pt) water
100g (4oz) rolled oats
40g (1½oz) flour
75g (3oz) butter or margarine
40g (1½oz) brown sugar
For serving:
custard

Date crunch pudding (serves 4–6)   colour page 83
POWER SETTING: NORMAL, FULL OR HIGH

1 Lightly grease a 17.5cm (7in) round, shallow microwave dish.
2 Place the dates and the water in a bowl, cover and cook for 5 min. Mash down with a fork and allow to cool.
3 Mix the oats with the flour. Cut up the butter or margarine, add to the dry ingredients and rub in until the mixture resembles coarse crumbs. Stir in the brown sugar.
4 Place half the oat mixture in the prepared dish and press down very firmly.
5 Spread the date mixture over this and cover with the second half of the oat mixture. Smooth over the top and press down lightly.
6 Cook uncovered for 5–6 min, giving a quarter turn every 1½ min. Allow to stand for 5 min.
7 Serve hot with custard.

Alternative conventional bake
Cook in a preheated oven at 200°C (400°F) Mark 6 for 20–25 min.

Fennel/Florence fennel

Fennel looks like a root but is the swollen base of the stems with the leaves removed. It is commonly used as a salad vegetable and has a strong aniseed flavour. When cooked, however, it loses some of its strong taste.

Fennel sauce *(serves 4)* *colour page 65*
POWER SETTING: NORMAL, FULL OR HIGH

This sauce makes a good accompaniment to salmon or mackerel

1 Cut the fennel into small pieces and cook with the salted water in a covered dish or boiling bag for 6–7 min. Drain off the juices and reserve.
2 Chop the fennel finely.
3 Melt the butter, add the flour and seasonings. Make the reserved juices up to 275ml (½pt) with milk and add gradually to the roux, stirring continuously. Stir in the fennel. (If preferred, the sauce may be puréed in a blender at this stage.)
4 Heat the sauce for 4–5 min until thickened and bubbling, stirring every 30 sec.
5 Allow the sauce to cool slightly and stir in the cream. Serve hot with fish.

1 medium head fennel, washed and trimmed
2 × 15ml tbsp (2tbsp) salted water
For the sauce:
15g (½oz) butter
15g (½oz) flour
salt and pepper
275ml (½pt) milk, approximately
3 × 15ml tbsp (3tbsp) single cream

Sauté fennel *(serves 6)*
POWER SETTING: NORMAL, FULL OR HIGH

1 Cut the fennel into 6mm (¼in) thick slices.
2 Melt half the butter in a dish, add the fennel slices and turn over in the butter. Add salt and pepper.
3 Cover the dish with a tightly fitting lid or clingfilm and cook for about 15 min, shaking or stirring twice throughout. Remove lid or clingfilm and cook uncovered for 1–2 min to evaporate any moisture from the fennel.
4 Place the fennel into a serving dish and keep warm.
5 Add the rest of the butter to the cooking dish and heat in the microwave until it bubbles and begins to foam.
6 Add lemon rind and juice and the herbs.
7 Pour over the fennel and serve hot.

3 heads fennel, washed and trimmed
75g (3oz) butter
salt and freshly ground black pepper
1 lemon, grated rind and juice
2 × 15ml tbsp (2tbsp) chopped mixed herbs

Figs

Although they can be hot-house grown in this country, most figs are imported. There are two main types of fresh fig – those with green skins and yellow-green flesh, and those with purple skins and red-purple flesh. Both types have a large number of small seeds and are used primarily as dessert or table fruits and eaten raw, although they can be lightly stewed and served with cream. Dried figs are used mainly in cooked sweet dishes and puddings.

450g (1lb) fresh figs
1 bottle white wine
4 × 15ml tbsp (4tbsp) clear honey
For serving:
cream

Figs in wine and honey *(serves 4)*
POWER SETTING: NORMAL, FULL OR HIGH AND DEFROST OR MEDIUM

1 Wash and dry the figs.
2 Place the wine in a large bowl or serving dish, cover and bring to the boil on normal, full or high setting in the microwave, about 8–10 min.
3 Add the figs to the wine with the honey, and simmer in the microwave on defrost or medium setting for 8–10 min until the figs are tender.
4 Remove the figs from the dish with a slotted spoon. Bring the wine up to the boil in the microwave on normal, full or high setting and cook until reduced by one-third.
5 Replace the figs into the syrup and leave to cool.
6 Chill before serving with cream.

75g (3oz) self-raising flour
75g (3oz) fresh brown breadcrumbs
75g (3oz) shredded suet
25g (1oz) soft brown sugar
pinch salt
175g (6oz) dried figs, chopped
50g (2oz) dates, chopped
25g (1oz) chopped almonds
1 lemon, grated rind and juice
2 eggs, beaten
2 × 5ml tsp (2tsp) black treacle
2 × 15ml tbsp (2tbsp) sherry
milk for mixing
For serving:
lemon foamy sauce (page 74)

Rich fig pudding *(serves 6)*   *colour page 83*
POWER SETTING: NORMAL, FULL OR HIGH

1 Lightly grease an 850ml (1½pt) pudding basin.
2 Sift the flour into a mixing bowl and add all the dry ingredients, fruit, nuts and lemon rind. Mix well together.
3 Add the lemon juice, eggs, black treacle and sherry and beat together into the dry ingredients. Add sufficient milk to make a soft mixture.
4 Place into the prepared pudding basin, smooth the top and cover with clingfilm. Make a slit with the pointed end of a sharp knife.
5 Cook for 6–8 min, turning once halfway through. Leave to stand for 5 min.
6 Invert onto a serving plate and serve hot with lemon foamy sauce.

Gooseberry Fool (page 70)

Gooseberries

Both dessert fruits and cooking fruits are available. Avoid any with bruised or damaged skins, and squashy fruits. Besides being used in fillings for pies and tarts, in jam making and fruit fools, gooseberries cooked as a sauce (below) make an excellent accompaniment to fish and poultry dishes.

450g (1lb) gooseberries, topped and tailed
sugar to taste
$1\frac{1}{2} \times$ 15ml tbsp ($1\frac{1}{2}$tbsp) custard powder
$1\frac{1}{2} \times$ 15ml tbsp ($1\frac{1}{2}$tbsp) caster sugar
275ml ($\frac{1}{2}$pt) milk
few drops green colouring, optional
150ml ($\frac{1}{4}$pt) double cream, whipped
For decoration:
$2 \times$ 15ml tbsp (2tbsp) cream
few sprigs mint or angelica leaves

Gooseberry fool *(serves 4–6)*   *colour page 69*
POWER SETTING: NORMAL, FULL OR HIGH

1 Wash the gooseberries and place in a roasting or boiling bag with sugar to taste.
2 Cook for 4–5 min until tender, shaking the bag once throughout. Leave to stand for a few minutes.
3 Mix the custard powder with the caster sugar. Blend in a little of the milk, then add the rest.
4 Cook uncovered for 3–4 min until bubbling and thick, stirring twice throughout.
5 Add to the gooseberries and put through a sieve or purée in a blender. Add a few drops of green colouring, if necessary, to give a pale-green tinge. Allow to cool slightly.
6 Stir in the double cream and pour into a serving dish or individual glasses.
7 Stir in a little cream over the top to give a swirled effect.
8 Chill before serving, decorated with mint or angelica leaves.

675g ($1\frac{1}{2}$lb) gooseberries
75–100g (3–4oz) sugar
25g (1oz) butter
$\frac{1}{2} \times$ 5ml tsp ($\frac{1}{2}$tsp) cinnamon
100g (4oz) plain flour
pinch salt
50g (2oz) rolled oats
75g (3oz) butter or margarine
100g (4oz) demerara sugar
For serving:
custard or cream

Gooseberry pie *(serves 4–6)*
POWER SETTING: NORMAL, FULL OR HIGH

1 Top and tail and wash the gooseberries. Place them in a 20–22.5cm (8–9in) dish with the sugar, butter and cinnamon. Cover and cook for 5–6 min until just soft. Drain off some of the juice and reserve.
2 Sift the flour with the salt. Stir in the rolled oats and rub in the butter or margarine. Stir in the demerara sugar. This will make a coarse crumb mixture.
3 Sprinkle the topping over the gooseberries and cook for 8–10 min until hot throughout and the topping is cooked. Turn two or three times throughout.
4 Serve hot or cold with custard or cream and hand the rest of the juice separately.

Alternative conventional bake
Cook in a preheated oven at 200°C (400°F) Mark 6 for 40–45 min.

225g (8oz) gooseberries, topped and tailed
90ml (3fl oz) water
$1–2 \times$ 15ml tbsp (1–2tbsp) caster sugar
25g (1oz) butter
$1 \times$ 15ml tbsp (1tbsp) chopped fennel *or*
$1 \times$ 5ml tsp (1tsp) ground fennel (both optional)

Gooseberry sauce *(makes about 275ml [$\frac{1}{2}$pt])*
POWER SETTING: NORMAL, FULL OR HIGH

This sauce is traditionally served with stuffed mackerel, but without the chopped fennel it goes very well with smoked mackerel instead of the more usual horseradish sauce, and may also be served with cold turkey or chicken

1 Place all the ingredients in a covered bowl or dish.
2 Cook for 3–4 min, shaking or stirring halfway through, or until the gooseberries pop open.
3 Serve hot or cold.

Grapefruit

The pale yellow grapefruit, usually with thick skin, is the largest of the citrus fruits. The flesh is slightly bitter in flavour but sweeter grapefruit with pink tinged flesh are sometimes available. Grapefruit are usually served cut in half and sprinkled with sugar as a breakfast or hors d'oeuvre dish, but can be used for marmalade making and in salads.

Citrus marmalade *(makes about 2½kg [5½lb])*
POWER SETTING: NORMAL, FULL OR HIGH

2 grapefruit
2 large lemons
2 oranges
850ml (1½pt) boiling water
1.8kg (4lb) preserving sugar

1 Wash, dry and halve the fruit. Squeeze out the juice and place it in a large glass bowl.
2 Remove the pith and pips from the fruit skins and tie them in a piece of muslin or fine cloth. Shred the peel according to your preference – fine, medium or coarse.
3 Place the peel in the bowl with the juice and the bag of pith and pips. Add 275ml (½pt) boiling water and leave to stand for 1 hour. Remove the bag.
4 Add the rest of the boiling water. Cover with clingfilm and cook for 20–30 min, depending on the thickness of the peel.
5 Add the sugar and stir until dissolved. Cook uncovered for 25–30 min, stirring every 5 min until setting point is reached.
6 Allow the marmalade to stand for 30 min, then pot, seal and label.

Grapefruit in brandy *(serves 4)*   *colour page 73*
POWER SETTING: NORMAL, FULL OR HIGH

3 large grapefruit, peeled
75g (3oz) demerara sugar
150ml (¼pt) water
1 × 5ml tsp (1tsp) cinnamon
3 × 15ml tbsp (3tbsp) brandy

A refreshing sweet course after a rich meal

1 Remove all the pith from the peeled grapefruit and carefully take out the core from the centre with a skewer. Cut the fruit into 1.25cm (½in) thick slices.
2 Add the sugar to the water with the cinnamon in a large, shallow dish.
3 Heat for 2 min, then stir until the sugar has dissolved in the water. Cook for a further 2 min, then lay the grapefruit slices into the syrup.
4 Cover and cook for 2–3 min, turning the slices over in the syrup halfway through.
5 Place the slices of grapefruit in a serving dish. Mix 3 × 15ml tbsp (3tbsp) of the syrup with the brandy and pour over the fruit.
6 Serve hot or chilled on their own.

Leeks

The delicate flavour of the leek resembles that of the onion. The white, tightly packed stem layers have dark green leaves at the top which are normally trimmed away. Leeks should be firm, straight and crisp; avoid those which have yellowing or discoloured leaves.

450g (1lb) small leeks, trimmed and washed

2 × 15ml tbsp (2tbsp) salted water

1 bay leaf

150ml (¼pt) olive oil

3–4 × 15ml tbsp (3–4tbsp) wine vinegar

salt and freshly ground black pepper

1 × 5ml tsp (1tsp) caster sugar

1 × 15ml tbsp (1tbsp) tomato purée

1 × 15ml tbsp (1tbsp) freshly chopped parsley

For garnish:
slices of hardboiled egg

Leeks vinaigrette (serves 4)   colour page 7
POWER SETTING: NORMAL, FULL OR HIGH

This dish can form part of a buffet party menu, but try serving it as an individual side salad with meat or fish instead of the more usual green or mixed salad

1 Slice the leeks thickly and place in a roasting or boiling bag or covered dish with the salted water and bay leaf.
2 Cook for 7–10 min, shaking or stirring twice throughout. Leave to stand for a few minutes.
3 Whisk the oil with the vinegar, seasoning and sugar. Beat in the tomato purée.
4 Drain the leeks, pour over the dressing and allow to cool.
5 Stir in the chopped parsley and serve chilled garnished with slices of hardboiled egg.

DO NOT FREEZE THIS DISH.

675g (1½lb) leeks, washed and trimmed

225g (8oz) potatoes, peeled

40g (1½oz) butter

1 stick celery, finely sliced

550ml (1pt) boiling chicken stock

salt and pepper

550ml (1pt) milk

275ml (½pt) double cream

freshly grated nutmeg

Vichysoisse soup (serves 4)
POWER SETTING: NORMAL, FULL OR HIGH

1 Slice the leeks finely and cut the potatoes into small dice.
2 Melt the butter for 1½ min, add the leeks, potatoes and celery. Mix well together, cover and cook for 5–6 min.
3 Pour on the boiling chicken stock, add salt and pepper. Cover and cook for 12–14 min, until the vegetables are tender.
4 Blend the mixture in a liquidiser or pass through a sieve.
5 Add the milk, cover and cook for 5–6 min until heated through.
6 Allow to cool, check seasoning and stir in the cream.
7 Serve chilled, sprinkled with freshly grated nutmeg.

DO NOT FREEZE THIS DISH WITH THE CREAM. FINISH JUST BEFORE SERVING.

450g (1lb) leeks, washed and trimmed

2 × 15ml tbsp (2tbsp) salted water

4 large, thin slices of ham

275ml (½pt) mornay sauce (page 30)

3 × 15ml tbsp (3tbsp) grated cheese

paprika pepper for sprinkling

Leek and ham rolls (serves 2 or 4)
POWER SETTING: NORMAL, FULL OR HIGH

Serve as a starter or main course

1 Cut the leeks in half lengthways, or if they are very large, cut into quarters.
2 Place the leek halves or quarters in a casserole dish with the salted water. Cover and cook for 7–10 min until tender. Drain well.
3 Keeping the leeks in strips, divide between the slices of ham. Roll up each slice and place back into the dish.
4 Cover and cook for 2 min until the ham is heated through.
5 Heat the mornay sauce, if necessary, and pour over the rolls.
6 Sprinkle with the grated cheese and paprika pepper and cook uncovered for 2–3 min until the cheese is melted. Alternatively, brown under a grill.
7 Serve hot, allowing 1 or 2 rolls per person, depending whether to be served as a starter or main course.

FREEZE THE SAUCE SEPARATELY.

Grapefruit in Brandy (page 71); Lemon Cheese Flan (page 74)

Lemons

Lemons are the most useful of all the citrus fruits, both rind and juice being used to flavour all kinds of dishes, whether sweet or savoury. The smaller thin-skinned, plump lemons normally have less peel and more juice than the larger, thick-skinned variety.

1l (1¾pt) jellied chicken stock
4 × 15ml tbsp (4tbsp) cooked rice
2 eggs
1 lemon, grated rind and juice
salt and freshly ground black pepper
For garnish:
a little finely grated lemon rind

Greek lemon soup *(serves 4)*   *colour page 53*
POWER SETTING: NORMAL, FULL OR HIGH

A refreshing starter

1 Heat the chicken stock in a large bowl until boiling, about 8–10 min. Add the rice.
2 Beat the eggs with the lemon rind and juice and seasoning.
3 Add a little of the hot stock to the eggs, beating well until smooth and then pour the mixture back into the stock, stirring continuously.
4 Heat without boiling for approximately 2–3 min, whisking every 15 sec to incorporate the egg mixture thoroughly into the stock.
5 Adjust seasoning and serve hot sprinkled with a little finely grated lemon rind.

225g (8oz) digestive biscuits, crumbed
25g (1oz) caster sugar
50g (2oz) butter, melted
For the filling:
225g (8oz) cream cheese
100g (4oz) lemon curd (page 75)
3 egg yolks, beaten
For decoration:
lemon twists

Lemon cheese flan *(serves 6)*   *colour page 73*
POWER SETTING: DEFROST OR MEDIUM

1 Reserving a third of the biscuit crumbs, mix the rest with the sugar. Add the melted butter and mix well together.
2 Press the mixture into the base and around the sides of a 20cm (8in) pie plate or flan dish. Chill in the refrigerator.
3 Cream the cheese and beat in the lemon curd. Add the egg yolks gradually, beating well after each addition.
4 Heat slowly on defrost or medium setting for 5 min, beating the mixture every minute until thick.
5 Pour into the chilled flan case and sprinkle with the reserved biscuit crumbs.
6 Serve chilled, decorated with lemon twists.

25g (1oz) butter or margarine
25g (1oz) caster sugar
1 lemon, grated rind and juice
1 egg, separated
25g (1oz) plain flour
150ml (¼pt) water

Lemon foamy sauce *(makes about 275ml [½pt])*
POWER SETTING: NORMAL, FULL OR HIGH

This light sauce can be served with sweet puddings

1 Cream the butter or margarine and caster sugar together until soft, beat in the lemon rind, egg yolk and flour.
2 Add the lemon juice to the water and gradually beat this into the creamed mixture. Do not worry if the mixture separates, as it will become smooth again as it cooks.
3 Heat for 2–3 min, stirring every 30 sec until thickened. If the sauce is too thick, add a little warm water and beat well.
4 Just before serving, whisk the egg white until it holds its shape and fold into the sauce.
5 If required hot, heat slowly until warmed through by giving 15–30 sec cooking at a time.

DO NOT FREEZE THIS DISH.

Lemon honey pudding (serves 5–6)
POWER SETTING: NORMAL, FULL OR HIGH

1 Lightly grease an 850ml (1½pt) pudding basin.
2 Cream the butter or margarine and caster sugar together until light.
3 Add the eggs gradually, beating well after each addition.
4 Sift the flour and salt together and fold into the creamed mixture. Stir in the breadcrumbs and grated lemon rind.
5 Fold in the lemon juice and sufficient hot water to make a soft mixture.
6 Place the honey in the bottom of the prepared basin and place the sponge mixture on top. Press down and smooth the top.
7 Cover with clingfilm slit with the pointed end of a sharp knife and cook for 6–7 min.
8 Leave to stand for 5 min before inverting onto a serving plate.
9 Serve hot with lemon foamy sauce and a little extra warmed honey.

100g (4oz) butter or margarine
100g (4oz) caster sugar
2 eggs, beaten
75g (3oz) self-raising flour
pinch salt
25g (1oz) fresh white breadcrumbs
1 lemon, grated rind and juice
1–2 × 15ml tbsp (1–2tbsp) hot water
3 × 15ml tbsp (3tbsp) clear honey
For serving:
lemon foamy sauce (page 74) and warmed honey

Lemon curd (makes about 1kg [2lb])
POWER SETTING: NORMAL, FULL OR HIGH

1 Cut the butter into pieces and place in a large bowl. Heat for 4–5 min until melted.
2 Beat together the rest of the ingredients and stir into the butter.
3 Cook uncovered for 6–7 min, stirring every minute until thick enough to coat the back of a wooden spoon.
4 Pour the curd into small jars, then seal and label.

Note: *Lemon curd does not keep well so is best made in small quantities and stored in a cool place for about 1 month.*

175g (6oz) butter
4 eggs
2 egg yolks
275g (10oz) caster sugar
4 large lemons, grated rind and juice

Lentils

Lentils are dried seeds of leguminous plants – similar to peas and beans – with a high protein content and are considered a good substitute for meat in the diet.

Lentil curry (serves 4)   colour page 11
POWER SETTING: NORMAL, FULL OR HIGH

1 Drain the lentils after soaking.
2 Melt the butter for 2 min, add the onions and garlic, toss well in the butter. Cover and cook for 5–6 min.
3 Stir in the curry powder and turmeric and cook for 1 min.
4 Add the lentils and boiling chicken stock. Cover and cook for 20–25 min until the lentils are tender. The consistency should be quite thick, but add a little extra boiling stock, if necessary, during the cooking period.
5 Add salt to taste and serve with meatballs or sausages.

225g (8oz) lentils, soaked for 2 hours
50g (2oz) butter
2 onions, peeled and chopped
2 cloves garlic, finely chopped
1 × 5ml tsp (1tsp) curry powder
½ × 5ml tsp (½tsp) turmeric
550ml (1pt) boiling chicken stock, approximately
salt to taste
For serving:
meatballs or sausages

Lentil patties *(serves 3–4)*
POWER SETTING: NORMAL, FULL OR HIGH

Make a well-flavoured thick lentil purée as given for lentil salad (below). When cold, adjust seasoning and stir in 1–2 × 15ml tbsp (1–2tbsp) freshly chopped parsley and a beaten egg to bind. Divide the mixture into 8 and form into patties between floured hands. Chill for 30 min or until set. Preheat a browning dish for $3\frac{1}{2}$–$4\frac{1}{2}$ min, add a little cooking oil and cook the patties for 2–3 min, turning over once halfway through. Drain on kitchen paper and serve hot with bacon or ham.

225g (8oz) lentils, soaked for 2 hours
1 small onion, peeled
6 cloves
1 bay leaf
1 bouquet garni
1 carrot, peeled and sliced
boiling salted water
stock, optional
150ml ($\frac{1}{4}$pt) french dressing (page 44)
1 clove garlic, crushed
For garnish:
tomato slices and onion rings

Lentil salad *(serves 4–6)*
POWER SETTING: NORMAL, FULL OR HIGH

Serve as an accompaniment to cold poultry or pork

1 Drain the lentils and place in a large bowl or casserole dish.
2 Stick the onion with the cloves and add to the lentils with the bay leaf, bouquet garni and carrot slices. Pour on boiling, salted water to cover.
3 Cover the dish and cook for 20–25 min until the lentils are tender. Drain and remove the onion, bay leaf and bouquet garni.
4 Sieve or purée the lentil mixture, adding a little stock if it is too thick. Allow to cool.
5 Beat in the french dressing and the garlic.
6 Serve cold garnished with tomato slices and onion rings.

Marrow

The marrow is a member of the gourd family and is best when young with white, delicate, tender flesh. Large marrows have a tendency towards being tough. On its own, marrow tends to be insipid and is, therefore, enhanced by well-flavoured stuffings or sauces.

2 × 15ml tbsp (2tbsp) oil
1 onion, peeled and finely chopped
450g (1lb) prepared marrow, cut into dice
225g (8oz) tomatoes, peeled and chopped
2 cloves garlic, crushed
salt and freshly ground black pepper

Marrow provençale *(serves 4)*
POWER SETTING: NORMAL, FULL OR HIGH

1 Place the oil in a bowl or serving dish with the onion. Toss well, cover and cook for 3 min.
2 Add the marrow, toss over so that it is well coated in the oil and onions, cover and cook for 8 min.
3 Add the tomatoes, garlic and seasoning to taste, cover and cook for 3–4 min. Stir well, cover and cook for a further 2–3 min.
4 Serve hot.

Melon with Port Jelly (page 79)

25g (1oz) butter

1 onion, peeled and finely chopped

1 clove garlic, finely chopped

450g (1lb) minced beef

salt and freshly ground black pepper

1 × 5ml tsp (1tsp) dried basil

few drops worcestershire sauce

225g (8oz) tomatoes, skinned and chopped

50g (2oz) mushrooms, chopped

75g (3oz) fresh white breadcrumbs

1 marrow, peeled, deseeded and cut into 8 rings

For serving:
jacket potatoes

Stuffed marrow rings *(serves 4)*

POWER SETTING: NORMAL, FULL OR HIGH

Serve as a main course

1 Melt the butter in a large bowl for 1 min. Add the onion and garlic, cover and cook for 3 min.
2 Add the mince and seasonings, cover and cook for 5 min, stirring once halfway through and breaking down any lumps with a fork.
3 Add the tomatoes, mushrooms and breadcrumbs, stir thoroughly and adjust seasoning to taste.
4 Arrange the marrow rings in a large casserole dish and fill the centre of each ring with the mince mixture. If necessary, make a second layer of rings in the dish.
5 Cover and cook for 25–30 min, turning twice throughout.
6 Serve hot with jacket potatoes.

Melons

This fruit with its crisp, sweet flesh is a member of the gourd family. There are many shapes and types available all through the year but when buying, check for ripeness by pressing gently at the stalk end.

Melon with port jelly (serves 4)   colour page 77
POWER SETTING: NORMAL, FULL OR HIGH

A really delicious, refreshing but simple starter

1 lemon table jelly to make 550ml (1pt)

150ml (¼pt) water

1 lemon, thinly pared rind and squeeze of juice

2.5cm (1in) cinnamon stick

275ml (½pt) port, approximately

2 small melons

For serving:
crushed ice and sprigs of mint or lemon twists

1 Break up the lemon table jelly into a bowl or measuring jug. Add the water, lemon rind and juice and cinnamon stick. Stir well.
2 Heat for about 1–1½ min, then stir until the jelly cubes are dissolved. Make up to 550ml (1pt) with the port and allow to cool.
3 Cut the melons in half, and remove a thin slice of the peel from the base of each half so that it will stand firm. Remove the seeds.
4 When the jelly is nearly cold, strain through a sieve and divide between the four halves of melon. Refrigerate until the jellies are set.
5 Serve on beds of crushed ice on individual serving plates or dishes. Garnish with sprigs of mint or lemon twists.

Note: *If there is any jelly left over, allow it to set, chop finely and pile into the centre of the melon halves.*

DO NOT FREEZE THIS DISH.

Mushrooms

These are available all the year round and are sold either as button, cap or flat mushrooms according to their age. The flat mushrooms are generally better in flavour than the buttons, and black and brown types are available with very little difference in taste. Choose dry, firm mushrooms and avoid any which look limp and shrivelled or sweaty.

Mushrooms à la Grecque (serves 6)   colour page 7
POWER SETTING: NORMAL, FULL OR HIGH

2 × 15ml tbsp (2tbsp) olive oil

1 small onion, peeled and finely chopped

1 clove garlic, crushed

450g (1lb) button mushrooms, whole or sliced

4 tomatoes, skinned and deseeded

salt and freshly ground black pepper

1 × 15ml tbsp (1tbsp) tomato purée

1 wine glass white wine

2 × 15ml tbsp (2tbsp) chopped parsley

1 Place the oil in a large serving dish with the onion and garlic. Cover and cook for 2 min.
2 Add the mushrooms, tomatoes, salt and freshly ground black pepper, cover and cook for 3 min.
3 Blend the tomato purée and wine together and add to the mushrooms. Stir, cover and cook for 2½ min.
4 Stir half the parsley into the dish and allow to cool, then chill for 2 hours.
5 Serve cold, sprinkled with the rest of the parsley.

Mushrooms au gratin *(serves 4)*
POWER SETTING: NORMAL, FULL OR HIGH

1 Melt the butter in a serving dish for 1 min. Add the mushrooms, season lightly, cover and cook for 5 min; leave to stand for a few minutes.
2 Heat the bèchamel sauce, if necessary, then stir in the cream.
3 Drain the mushrooms and spoon the sauce over. Mix the breadcrumbs with the cheese and sprinkle over the top of the sauce. Heat in the microwave for 2–3 min until the cheese is melted. Alternatively, brown under a hot grill.
4 Serve immediately.

FREEZE THE SAUCE SEPARATELY. FINISH WITH THE BREADCRUMBS AND CHEESE JUST BEFORE SERVING.

25g (1oz) butter
450g (1lb) button mushrooms, washed and sliced
salt and pepper
275ml ($\frac{1}{2}$pt) bèchamel sauce (page 40)
150ml ($\frac{1}{4}$pt) single cream
3 × 15ml tbsp (3tbsp) browned breadcrumbs
3 × 15ml tbsp (3tbsp) grated cheddar and parmesan cheese, mixed

Mushroom-stuffed cannelloni *(serves 4)*
POWER SETTING: NORMAL, FULL OR HIGH

Serve as a main dish or as a starter course

1 Place 2 × 15ml tbsp (2tbsp) of the oil in a large bowl, add the onions and garlic, toss well, cover and cook for 2$\frac{1}{2}$ min.
2 Add the mushrooms, herbs and seasoning, cover and cook for 3 min. Stir in the tomatoes.
3 Cook the cannelloni in a large, covered bowl of boiling, salted water with the remaining 1 × 15ml tbsp (1tbsp) oil for 5–6 min. Drain the pasta and rinse in cold water.
4 Fill the cannelloni with the mushroom mixture and place in a serving dish.
5 Heat the bèchamel sauce, if necessary, and stir in half the cheese. Spoon the sauce over the cannelloni. Sprinkle with the rest of the cheese and paprika pepper.
6 Cook for 3–4 min until heated through and serve, handing more parmesan cheese separately.

3 × 15ml tbsp (3tbsp) oil
1 onion, peeled and finely chopped
2 cloves garlic, finely chopped
100g (4oz) mushrooms, chopped
1 × 5ml tsp (1tsp) dried sweet basil
salt and freshly ground black pepper
4 tomatoes, skinned and chopped
8 cannelloni tubes
275ml ($\frac{1}{2}$pt) bèchamel sauce (page 40)
25g (1oz) grated parmesan cheese
paprika pepper for sprinkling

Creamed mushrooms and peas *(serves 4)*   *colour page 103*
POWER SETTING: NORMAL, FULL OR HIGH

1 Remove the rinds from the bacon and cut each rasher into strips.
2 Place the bacon strips into a serving dish, cover and cook for 2 min. Add the mushrooms, toss well in the fat from the bacon, cover and cook for 5–6 min.
3 Place the frozen peas in a bowl, cover and cook for 2$\frac{1}{2}$ min. Add salt, pepper and herbs, toss well, cover and cook for 2$\frac{1}{2}$–3$\frac{1}{2}$ min. Drain.
4 Add the peas to the mushrooms and bacon. Stir in the cream and adjust seasoning.
5 Cook for 30–60 sec until just heated through without boiling.
6 Serve garnished with triangles of toasted or fried bread.

4 large rashers bacon
225g (8oz) button mushrooms, washed and sliced
350g (12oz) frozen peas
salt and freshly ground black pepper
pinch mixed herbs
150ml ($\frac{1}{4}$pt) double cream
For serving:
triangles of toasted or fried bread

Tomato-stuffed Peppers (page 97); Spinach Gratinée (page 110); Mushroom-stuffed Cannelloni (above)

Nuts

The number of recipes which call for nuts in the list of ingredients for both savoury and sweet dishes must surely be endless, so I have included here just two recipes which could assist the vegetarian menu.

25g (1oz) butter

25g (1oz) flour

150ml (¼pt) milk

100g (4oz) minced nuts

50g (2oz) fresh brown breadcrumbs

2 × 5ml tsp (2tsp) finely grated raw onion

½ egg

1 × 5ml tsp (1tsp) chopped parsley

½ × 5ml tsp (½tsp) mixed dried herbs

1 × 5ml tsp (1tsp) lemon juice

salt and pepper

beaten egg and breadcrumbs for coating

oil for frying

For serving:

tomato sauce (page 114) or salad

Nut cutlets *(serves 3 or 6)*

POWER SETTING: NORMAL, FULL OR HIGH

1 Melt the butter for 1 min, stir in the flour and blend well together. Stir in the milk gradually and cook for 2 min, stirring every 30 sec until thickened. Beat well.

2 Stir in the nuts, breadcrumbs, onion, egg, herbs and lemon juice. Season to taste.

3 Turn the mixture onto a plate, smooth out and mark into 6 equal portions. Leave to cool, then refrigerate until cold.

4 Shape the portions into cutlets, patties or croquettes. Coat in beaten egg and dip into breadcrumbs.

5 Preheat a browning dish for 7 min, add 2 × 15ml tbsp (2tbsp) oil and heat for 30 sec.

6 Place the cutlets into the dish, cover and cook for 3–4 min, turning the cutlets over once halfway through. Drain on kitchen paper towel.

7 Serve hot with tomato sauce or cold with salad.

225g (8oz) minced nuts

450g (1lb) boiled rice

50g (2oz) fat

1 × 15ml tbsp (1tbsp) chopped celery

1 onion, finely chopped

2 × 5ml tsp (2tsp) yeast extract

salt and pepper

1 × 15ml tbsp (1tbsp) chopped parsley

2 eggs, beaten

2 × 15ml tbsp (2tbsp) tomato sauce

For garnish:

sprigs of parsley

For serving:

tomato sauce (page 114)

Nut Cutlets (above); Date Crunch Pudding (page 66); Rich Fig Pudding (page 68)

Savoury nut loaf *(serves 4)*

POWER SETTING: NORMAL, FULL OR HIGH

1 Mix the nuts and rice together.

2 Melt the fat for 1 min in a bowl, add the celery and onion, toss well in the fat, cover and cook for 2–3 min until soft.

3 Mix the yeast extract into the onion and celery and add to the nuts and rice.

4 Add salt and pepper to taste and the parsley. Bind together with the eggs and tomato sauce.

5 Place in a lightly greased microwave loaf dish. Cover and cook for 9 min. Leave to stand for a few minutes before turning out onto a serving plate or dish.

6 Pour a little tomato sauce over the nut loaf and garnish with sprigs of parsley. Serve hot, with the rest of the sauce handed separately.

Okra

Okra, or ladies' fingers, are green vegetables shaped like small carrots with furry skins which contain seeds. They may be cooked whole or cut into 2.5cm (1in) lengths and served tossed in butter or with hollandaise sauce (page 33).

25g (1oz) butter

1 onion, peeled and sliced

225g (8oz) okra, washed and sliced

225g (8oz) aubergine, trimmed and sliced

2 large tomatoes, skinned and chopped

salt and freshly ground black pepper

For garnish:
chopped parsley

Okra with aubergine *(serves 4)*
POWER SETTING: NORMAL, FULL OR HIGH

1 Melt the butter for 1 min in a large bowl or dish. Add the onion, toss well in the butter, cover and cook for 2 min.
2 Add the okra, aubergine, tomatoes and seasonings, cover and cook for 8–10 min until the vegetables are tender.
3 Serve hot sprinkled with chopped parsley.

450g (1lb) okra, washed

2 × 15ml tbsp (2tbsp) salted water

2 × 15ml tbsp (2tbsp) oil

2 onions, peeled and minced

2 green chillies, minced

1 clove garlic, minced

2.5cm (1in) root ginger, minced

1 × 15ml tbsp (1tbsp) ground coriander

1 × 5ml tsp (1tsp) turmeric

40g (1½oz) creamed coconut

2 tomatoes, skinned and quartered

salt to taste

For serving:
cooked rice and natural yoghurt

Okra curry *(serves 4–6)*   *colour page 11*
POWER SETTING: NORMAL, FULL OR HIGH

1 Cook the prepared okra in the salted water in a boiling or roasting bag or covered dish for 8 min, drain.
2 Place the oil and the onions in a covered bowl or dish and toss over well. Cook for about 5 min until transparent. Add the chillies, garlic and ginger, cover and cook for 3 min.
3 Stir in the coriander and turmeric, cook for 1 min.
4 Add the coconut, tomatoes and okra, stir well, cover and cook for 5–6 min until tender and the flavours are blended. Adjust seasoning.
5 Serve hot with cooked rice and yoghurt.

Note: *Creamed coconut is pure coconut which has been processed into a solid cream. It is available from health food shops and delicatessens.*

Onions

Onions are one of the popular vegetables used for flavouring and vary from round to flat-shaped bulbs. Spanish onions were originally from Spain but the name is now given to any large onion with a mild flavour. Spring onions are available all the year round and although principally used in salads, they also give a good flavour to cooked dishes.

Casserole of onions and mushrooms (*serves 4*)
POWER SETTING: NORMAL, FULL OR HIGH

1 Place the onions in a large bowl or casserole dish, pour on sufficient boiling water to cover.
2 Cover the dish and bring the water back up to the boil in the microwave. Drain.
3 Melt 25g (1oz) butter in the dish for about 1 min, add the onions and toss in the butter. Cover and cook for 5–6 min until tender.
4 Using a slotted spoon, remove the onions from the dish onto a plate and keep warm.
5 Place the mushrooms in the bowl with the butter and juices from the onions. Toss over, cover and cook for 5–6 min.
6 Using a slotted spoon, remove the mushrooms from the dish and place with the onions.
7 Melt 15g ($\frac{1}{2}$oz) butter for 30 sec, add the flour to the dish and blend with the butter. Add the milk gradually, then cook for 3–4 min until thickened and bubbling. Add salt and pepper to taste and stir in the cream.
8 Reserve 3–4 cooked mushrooms and add the remainder with the onions to the sauce. Chop the reserved mushrooms finely and add to the sauce. Mix well together.
9 Heat through without boiling for $1\frac{1}{2}$–2 min.
10 Serve hot, sprinkled with grated nutmeg.

225g (8oz) button onions, peeled
boiling water
40g (1½oz) butter
225g (8oz) button mushrooms, washed
25g (1oz) plain flour
275ml (½pt) milk
salt and pepper
2 × 15ml tbsp (2tbsp) double cream
grated nutmeg for sprinkling

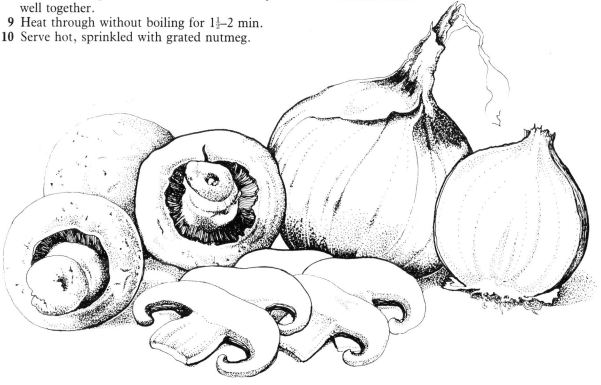

50g (2oz) butter
450g (1lb) onions, peeled and
thinly sliced
25g (1oz) flour
salt and freshly ground black
pepper
1 × 5ml tsp (1tsp) sugar
550ml (1pt) boiling beef stock
For serving:
4 slices french bread, toasted
grated cheese

French onion soup (*serves 4*)
POWER SETTING: NORMAL, FULL OR HIGH

1 Heat the butter in a large, shallow serving dish for 2 min. Toss the onion in the butter and cook for 5 min.
2 Add the flour and mix into the butter and onion. Add salt and pepper to taste and the sugar.
3 Add the stock gradually, mix well together. Cover and cook for 25 min.
4 Place the toasted bread on top of the soup and sprinkle with the grated cheese.
5 Heat in the microwave for 2–3 min until the cheese is melted or alternatively, brown the cheese under a hot grill.
6 Serve immediately.

Note: *For a 'special' soup, 2 × 15ml tbsp (2tbsp) brandy may be added to the cooked soup before garnishing with the toast and cheese.*

DO NOT FREEZE THIS DISH WITH THE TOAST. ADD WITH THE CHEESE JUST BEFORE SERVING.

2 large onions, peeled and
finely sliced
3 × 15ml tbsp (3tbsp) oil or
dripping
caster sugar for dusting

Fried onions (*serves 3–4*)
POWER SETTING: NORMAL, FULL OR HIGH

1 Push the onion slices through to form rings.
2 Heat the oil or dripping for 2–3 min in a large bowl. Toss in the onion rings so that they are well coated in the oil.
3 Cover and cook for 5 min, stir well and dust with a little caster sugar. Cover and cook for 3–4 min until tender.
4 Serve hot with sausages or steaks.

Note: *Alternatively, the onions may be cooked in a browning dish which has been preheated for 5 min. Add the onion rings which have been tossed in the oil or dripping, cover and cook for 6–7 min, tossing the onions over once halfway through.*

450g (1lb) button onions or
shallots
boiling water
25g (1oz) butter
2 × 15ml tbsp (2tbsp) caster
sugar

Glazed onions (*serves 4–5*)   *colour page 15*
POWER SETTING: NORMAL, FULL OR HIGH

1 Peel the onions and place in a large bowl or casserole dish. Pour on sufficient boiling water to cover.
2 Cover the dish and bring the water up to the boil in the microwave, drain and place the onions back into the dish.
3 Add the butter to the onions, cover and cook for 5 min. Shake the dish to stir the onions and sprinkle with the caster sugar.
4 Cook uncovered for 3–4 min until tender and glazed.
5 Serve hot.

French Onion Soup (above); Cassoulet (page 42)

Oranges

These globe-shaped fruits are available all the year round, although the bitter seville oranges, which are mainly used in marmalade making, are imported from Spain during January and February. The thick-skinned oranges are easier to peel and, like the navel and valencia oranges, have few pips. Oranges may be used as dessert fruits or in cooking; the grated rind and juice are used widely as flavourings for many dishes.

Mulled oranges *(serves 4)*
POWER SETTING: NORMAL, FULL OR HIGH

225g (8oz) caster sugar
150ml ($\frac{1}{4}$pt) water
red wine, $\frac{1}{3}$ bottle, approximately
1 clove
2.5cm (1in) cinnamon stick
$\frac{1}{2}$ orange, thinly pared rind
$\frac{1}{2}$ lemon, thinly pared rind
4 large oranges
For serving:
cream

1 Combine sugar, water, 150ml ($\frac{1}{4}$pt) red wine, clove, cinnamon, orange and lemon peel in a bowl.
2 Bring to the boil in the microwave and cook uncovered until reduced and syrupy, about 8–10 min. Remove the clove, peel and cinnamon stick and add 2 × 15ml tbsp (2tbsp) red wine.
3 Peel the oranges. Either divide the fruit into segments or cut into thin slices, removing all excess membrane.
4 Place the oranges in the hot syrup and allow to cool.
5 Chill before serving with cream.

Orange flower dessert *(serves 4)*   colour page 91
POWER SETTING: NORMAL, FULL OR HIGH

2 × 15ml tbsp (2tbsp) caster sugar
3 × 5ml tsp (3tsp) cornflour
4 × 15ml tbsp (4tbsp) water
150ml ($\frac{1}{4}$pt) orange juice
$\frac{1}{2}$ × 5ml tsp ($\frac{1}{2}$tsp) finely grated orange rind
2 × 15ml tbsp (2tbsp) cointreau
1 × 15ml tbsp (1tbsp) brandy
1 × 5ml tsp (1tsp) butter
4 thin-skinned oranges
For decoration:
whipped cream
sprigs of mint or angelica leaves

1 Mix the sugar and cornflour together in a small bowl. Blend with the water and add the orange juice and rind. Mix well together.
2 Cook for 2–3 min, stirring every 30 sec until thickened. Add the liqueurs and butter, beating well.
3 Score through the skin of each orange lengthways, making 8 cuts from the top to almost the base.
4 Carefully peel back each segment of skin, and loosen the orange segments, removing any excess membrane and pith from the skin and the orange.
5 Fold each segment of peel inwards so the tip fits under the base of the orange. Place into individual serving glasses.
6 Brush the orange flesh with the glaze.
7 Serve chilled, add a little more glaze to the oranges and decorate with a swirl of piped cream and sprigs of mint or angelica leaves.

DO NOT FREEZE THIS DISH.

St Clementine sorbet (serves 4–6)   colour page 99
POWER SETTING: NORMAL, FULL OR HIGH

1 Mix the grated rinds and juices together and make up to 700ml (1¼pt) with cold water.
2 Place in a large bowl with the caster sugar.
3 Cover and bring to the boil in the microwave, about 9–10 min.
4 Stir in the gelatine until dissolved and leave to cool. Place in the freezer and leave until almost hard.
5 Whisk the egg whites until stiff and beat into the orange and lemon mixture.
6 Place into containers and freeze.

Note: *Remove from the freezer about ½ hour before required.*

1 orange, grated rind and juice
1 lemon, grated rind and juice
cold water
50g (2oz) caster sugar
1 × 5ml tsp (1tsp) gelatine
2 egg whites

Oranges in caramel (serves 4–8)
POWER SETTING: NORMAL, FULL OR HIGH

1 Finely grate the rind from 3 oranges. Remove peel, pith and cut membrane from all the oranges.
2 Slice the oranges thinly, reserving any juices. Reshape each orange with the slices and secure with a cocktail stick. Place the oranges into a serving dish.
3 Add the sugar to the cold water with the liqueur and juice from the oranges. Bring to the boil in the microwave and, without stirring, cook until a light golden brown, about 10–12 min.
4 Quickly add the hot water to the caramel. (Be careful to avoid the steam; protect your hand with an ovenglove or towel if necessary.)
5 Return to the microwave and heat for 30 sec. Stir well and leave to cool.
6 Pour the cooled caramel over the oranges in the serving dish and sprinkle with the grated orange rind.
7 Serve cold with whipped cream.

8 oranges
225g (8oz) granulated sugar
150ml (¼pt) cold water
1 × 15ml tbsp (1tbsp) grand marnier or cointreau, optional
150ml (¼pt) hot water
For serving:
whipped cream

8 pancakes (see below)

For the filling:

2 oranges

3–4 × 15ml tbsp (3tbsp) honey

2 lemons, juice

Orange and honey pancakes *(serves 4 or 8)*

POWER SETTING: NORMAL, FULL OR HIGH

The citrus fruits and honey make a delicious but not too sweet filling for the pancakes

1 Make the pancakes and cover to keep warm.
2 Peel the oranges and remove all the pith and outer membrane. Divide the fruit into segments, reserving any juice.
3 Place the orange juice, honey and lemon juice into a large, shallow, round dish and heat for 1½–2 min. Stir until well blended.
4 Reserve a few of the orange segments and divide the rest between the 8 pancakes. Fold each pancake into quarters.
5 Place the pancakes into the dish with the sauce, overlapping slightly if necessary.
6 Cover the dish and heat through for 2–3 min, turning the dish once halfway through.
7 Serve hot, decorated with the reserved orange segments.

100g (4oz) plain flour

pinch salt

1 egg, beaten

275ml (½pt) milk

oil for frying

Pancakes

Pancakes cannot be successfully cooked in the microwave, so are best cooked conventionally; this basic pancake batter is sufficient to make 8–10 thin pancakes

1 Sift the flour and salt into a mixing bowl. Make a well in the centre and drop in the beaten egg.
2 Slowly pour on half the milk, mixing the egg and milk into the flour with a wooden spoon.
3 Beat the mixture with a wooden spoon or whisk until smooth and free of lumps.
4 Add the remaining milk, whisking continually until the mixture is bubbly and the consistency of single cream.
5 Heat a 17.5–20cm (7–8in) frying pan on a conventional hotplate or burner. Just sufficient oil should be added to prevent the pancakes from sticking.
6 The pan and oil should be really hot. Pour in just enough batter to allow a thin film to coat the base of the pan, tilting the pan to spread the mixture.
7 The base of the pancake should be cooked in about 1 min. Flip the pancake over with a palette knife or spatula and cook the other side for about 1 min. If the pancakes are taking too long to cook, adjust the heat or make sure that too much batter is not being used.
8 Layer the pancakes in absorbent kitchen paper and keep warm if to be used immediately. Alternatively, leave to cool, or freeze as they may be thawed and reheated most satisfactorily in the microwave.
9 Fill and use as required, allowing one per person if served as a starter to a meal or two if served as a snack or as a main course with vegetables.

Note: *The ingredients for the pancake batter may be blended in a liquidiser or food processor.*

Orange and Honey Pancakes (above); Orange Flower Dessert (page 88)

Parsnips

This winter root vegetable is available from October and is normally better after the first frosts. The roots should be crisp and clean, avoid any with soft brown patches on the skin. The creamy white flesh is somewhat sweet with a slightly aromatic flavour.

450g (1lb) parsnips, peeled
2 × 15ml tbsp (2tbsp) salted water
40g (1½oz) butter
freshly ground black pepper

Buttered parsnips *(serves 4)*   *colour page 15*
POWER SETTING: NORMAL, FULL OR HIGH

1 Cut the parsnips into slices or quarters, depending on their size. If very large, cut into dice. Cut out and discard the core if woody.
2 Place the parsnips with the salted water into a casserole dish. Cover and cook for 8–10 min until tender. Drain well.
3 Add the butter to the hot parsnips, toss over until the butter is melted and the parsnips are coated in the butter.
4 Cook uncovered for 1½–2 min to evaporate any moisture.
5 Sprinkle with freshly ground black pepper and serve hot.

Creamed parsnips

Use the ingredients and method for buttered parsnips, but mash the parsnips with a fork or potato masher before stirring in the butter. Two or three tablespoons of single cream or top of the milk may be added before sprinkling with freshly ground black pepper.

Sauté parsnips

Use the ingredients and method for buttered parsnips. When the butter is added, toss into a browning dish which has been preheated for about 5 min, to brown the outside of the parsnips. Serve hot, sprinkled with freshly ground black pepper.

Note: *The above recipes are also suitable for swedes.*

Peaches

These stone fruit with velvety skins vary in size, also in colour from deep pink to red and golden. Freestone peaches are not often available but have the best flavour with soft, juicy flesh which comes away from the stone easily. Clingstone peaches have a yellow or golden flesh which is firm and more difficult to remove from the stone.

Peaches and cream pie *(serves 8–10)*
POWER SETTING: DEFROST OR MEDIUM

1 Halve and slice the peaches and arrange in the bottom of a 22.5cm (9in) dish. Sprinkle with caster sugar (use less if the peaches are canned) and the cinnamon.
2 Beat the eggs with the soured cream and pour over the peaches. Cook for 12–15 min on defrost or medium setting until set, giving a quarter turn every 3 min.
3 Mix together the flours and salt. Rub in the butter and stir in the demerara sugar to give a coarse crumb mixture.
4 Sprinkle the crumb mixture over the peaches and cook on defrost or medium setting for 7–8 min until the crumb topping is cooked.
5 Leave to cool slightly and serve with whipped cream, or when cold pipe with whipped cream.

Alternative conventional bake
Add the eggs and the cream to the peaches, scatter with the topping and cook in a preheated oven at 180°C (350°F) Mark 4 for 50–60 min.

DO NOT FREEZE THIS DISH.

900g (2lb) peaches, fresh or canned, drained
50–100g (2–4oz) caster sugar
$\frac{1}{2}$ × 5ml tsp ($\frac{1}{2}$tsp) cinnamon
2 eggs, beaten
150ml ($\frac{1}{4}$pt) soured cream
25g (1oz) plain flour
50g (2oz) wholemeal flour
pinch salt
75g (3oz) butter
75g (3oz) demerara sugar
For decoration:
whipped cream

Peaches with raspberry purée *(serves 4)* *colour page 39*
POWER SETTING: NORMAL, FULL OR HIGH

1 Skin the peaches by heating each one in the microwave for 15–30 sec to enable the skin to be peeled off easily.
2 Place the peaches in a casserole dish and sprinkle with the caster sugar, water and kirsch.
3 Cover and cook for about 5 min until tender, turning the peaches over or basting with the juices twice throughout. Allow to stand for a few minutes.
4 Purée the raspberries in a blender or pass through a sieve. Add the juices from the peaches to the purée and adjust sugar to taste.
5 Serve the peaches hot or cold in individual glasses or dishes with a little raspberry purée poured over; hand the rest separately with the cream or ice cream for serving.

4 medium peaches
25–50g (1–2oz) caster sugar
1 × 15ml tbsp (1tbsp) water
1 × 15ml tbsp (1tbsp) kirsch
225g (8oz) raspberries, fresh or frozen
For serving:
cream or ice cream

Stuffed peaches *(serves 4)*
POWER SETTING: NORMAL, FULL OR HIGH

1 Skin the peaches by heating each one in the microwave for 15–30 sec to enable the skin to be peeled off easily.
2 Cut the peaches in half and remove the stones. Scoop out a little more of the flesh and chop finely. Cover and cook the peach halves for 3–4 min.
3 Mix the cake and macaroon crumbs with the caster sugar and the chopped peach flesh.
4 Melt the butter in a small bowl for 1 min and add this to the crumb mixture with the egg yolk to bind.
5 Divide the mixture between the peach halves and place in a serving dish.
6 Cover and cook for 2–3 min, turning the dish halfway through. Sprinkle with grated nutmeg.
7 Serve hot or cold with cream.

4 large peaches
50g (2oz) cake crumbs
50g (2oz) macaroon biscuits, crumbed
1 × 5ml tsp (1tsp) caster sugar
25g (1oz) butter
1 egg yolk
grated nutmeg for sprinkling
For serving:
whipped cream

Note: *Canned peaches may be used, in which case the first cooking time is not necessary.*

Pears

Pears are a popular fruit and, like apples, can be divided into cooking and dessert varieties. Cooking pears are not acid but are very often lacking in flavour and are best cooked in syrup or wine. Dessert pears are sweet and juicy; they must be handled with care as they bruise easily. It is better to buy them when slightly firm as they will ripen quickly at room temperature.

275ml (½pt) cider or white wine
sugar to taste
1 orange, grated rind
2.5cm (1in) cinnamon stick
½ × 5ml tsp (½tsp) grated nutmeg
4 cooking pears
For serving:
cream

Baked pears in cider *(serves 4)*
POWER SETTING: NORMAL, FULL OR HIGH

1 Place the cider or wine, sugar, orange rind and spices in a large dish, cover and bring to the boil in the microwave then cook for 2 min.
2 Peel the pears and cut in half lengthways. Remove the cores and place the pear halves, cut side down, into the cider or white wine. Cover and cook for about 5 min or until tender.
3 Remove the pears and boil the cider or wine in the microwave until slightly reduced.
4 Replace the pears into the dish and leave to cool.
5 Serve cool or chilled with whipped cream.

4 large ripe dessert pears
15g (½oz) blanched almonds, chopped
15g (½oz) glacé cherries, chopped
6g (¼oz) angelica, chopped
100g (4oz) dark plain chocolate
3 × 15ml tbsp (3tbsp) strong black coffee
25g (1oz) butter
1 egg, separated
1 × 15ml tbsp (1tbsp) rum or brandy
For decoration:
angelica leaves
For serving:
whipped cream

Chocolate pears *(serves 4)*
POWER SETTING: NORMAL, FULL OR HIGH

1 Peel the pears and remove cores from the base. Cut a small slice from the base so that the pears will stand upright in their serving dish; leave the stalks intact.
2 Mix together the almonds, glacé cherries and angelica and place a little of this mixture into the core cavities.
3 Break up the chocolate and place into a bowl with the black coffee.
4 Heat for about 4 min until the chocolate is melted. Beat well to combine with the coffee, then beat in the butter, egg yolk and the rum or brandy. Allow to cool slightly.
5 Whisk the egg white until stiff and fold into the chocolate until smooth.
6 Spoon the sauce over the pears so they are evenly coated then chill in the refrigerator.
7 Decorate the pears with angelica leaves placed each side of the stalks.
8 Serve chilled with whipped cream piped around the base of each pear.

DO NOT FREEZE THIS DISH.

Peas

The early varieties are the mange-tout or sugar peas with flat, edible pods and very small peas inside. They should be topped and tailed and cooked in a little salted water. Drain thoroughly and toss in melted butter with pepper and salt to taste. They may also be served with a cream sauce. This delicious vegetable makes an ideal starter course or accompanying vegetable to a main course.

The later varieties of peas must be shelled from the pods which should be crisp and bright in colour.

Chocolate Pears (above)

225g (8oz) dried split peas, soaked overnight

15g (½oz) butter

1 egg, optional

salt and pepper

For serving:
boiled ham

Pease pudding (*serves 4*)

POWER SETTING: NORMAL, FULL OR HIGH

1 After soaking, cook the peas in a covered bowl or dish in plenty of boiling water for 45–50 min in the microwave, until tender.
2 Drain well, then mash, sieve or blend in a liquidiser with the butter, the egg, if used, and seasoning.
3 Place the mixture in a cloth or muslin and cook with the ham for the last 5 min of microwave cooking time.
4 Turn the pudding out of the cloth before serving.

Note: *Soak the ham for 24 hours or at least overnight, changing the water occasionally. Allow 7–9 min per 450g (1lb) for the ham, weighed after soaking. Normally no water is required for 'boiling' but if preferred, add 150–275ml (¼–½pt) boiling water to the dish. Cover the dish and cook for half the cooking time, allow to stand for 20 min, then turn the joint over, cover and continue to cook for the rest of the time. If the joint is large, a further resting period of 20–30 min may be required at the end of the cooking time.*

25g (1oz) butter

1 small onion, peeled and finely chopped

100g (4oz) ham, diced

450g (1lb) cooked peas, fresh or frozen

275ml (½pt) single cream

salt and freshly ground black pepper

2 × 15ml tbsp (2tbsp) finely grated parmesan cheese

2 × 15ml tbsp (2tbsp) finely grated gruyère cheese

paprika pepper for sprinkling

Peas au gratin (*serves 4*)

POWER SETTING: NORMAL, FULL OR HIGH

1 Melt the butter in a bowl for 1 min, add the onion, cover and cook for 1½ min; add the ham and continue to cook for 2–3 min.
2 Mix in the peas, cover and cook for 3 min.
3 Warm the cream for 1–1½ min, stirring every 30 sec.
4 Combine the cream with the peas and ham mixture, adjust seasoning.
5 Sprinkle with the grated cheeses. Heat for 2–3 min until the cheeses are melted and sprinkle with paprika pepper. Alternatively, brown the dish under a hot grill.
6 Serve hot.

DO NOT FREEZE THIS DISH.

450g (1lb) green peas

12–14 spring onions

2 × 15ml tbsp (2tbsp) salted water

8–10 outer lettuce leaves, washed and shredded

1 sprig of mint

25g (1oz) butter

1 × 5ml tsp (1tsp) caster sugar

freshly ground black pepper

Peas with lettuce and spring onions (*serves 4–6*)

POWER SETTING: NORMAL, FULL OR HIGH

1 Place the peas in a bowl or serving dish. Cut the spring onions into even lengths, wash and add to the peas. Pour on the salted water, cover and cook for 5–6 min.
2 Add the shredded lettuce leaves and the mint, stir, cover and cook for 2–4 min until the peas are tender.
3 Drain off the water, add the butter and caster sugar to taste and cook for 2 min, stirring well after 1 min.
4 Adjust seasoning and serve hot.

DO NOT FREEZE THIS DISH.

Peppers

Green, red and golden peppers are available. They are excellent for use in salads, but lend themselves particularly well to stuffing with a variety of meat or fish mixtures. Peppers should be crisp and shiny; the stalk end should be sliced off to allow removal of the inner membranes and seeds.

Tomato-stuffed peppers *(serves 4)*   *colour page 80*
POWER SETTING: NORMAL, FULL OR HIGH

This pepper dish is of Italian origin and is served cold as a starter

1 Cut the peppers in half lengthways and remove the core and seeds. Place in a large casserole dish.
2 Cover and cook the peppers for 4 min, turn the pepper halves, cook for 3–4 min.
3 Mix together the tomatoes, garlic, anchovies and breadcrumbs. Add sufficient olive oil to combine the ingredients, and add seasonings to taste.
4 Divide the mixture between the peppers, dot with butter, cover and cook for 5–6 min.
5 Serve cold, sprinkled with chopped parsley.

Note: *Tuna fish can replace the anchovies if preferred.*

4 medium red or green peppers
6 large tomatoes, peeled and chopped
1–2 cloves garlic, finely chopped
50g (2oz) can anchovy fillets, drained and chopped
4 × 15ml tbsp (4tbsp) dry breadcrumbs
2 × 15ml tbsp (2tbsp) olive oil
salt and freshly ground black pepper
2 × 15ml tbsp (2tbsp) butter
For garnish:
chopped parsley

Stuffed peppers *(serves 2)*
POWER SETTING: NORMAL, FULL OR HIGH

1 Cut a slice from the top of each pepper. Remove the core and seeds. Reserve the slice to use as a lid.
2 Cover and cook the peppers for 2 min, turn them over, cook for 2 min.
3 Place the rice in a bowl or dish, stir in the boiling chicken stock, onion, seasoning and bay leaf.
4 Cover and cook for 5 min, stir and cook for a further 3–5 min or until all the stock is absorbed. Remove the bay leaf.
5 Add the ham and sultanas to the rice. Fill the peppers with the rice mixture and replace the lids.
6 Stand the peppers in the serving dish, cover and cook for 3 min. Serve with a little extra boiled rice.

2 medium green peppers
50g (2oz) long grain rice
165ml ($\frac{1}{3}$pt) boiling chicken stock
1 onion, peeled and finely chopped
salt and pepper
1 bay leaf
50g (2oz) cooked ham or chicken, chopped
40g (1$\frac{1}{2}$oz) sultanas
For serving:
plain boiled rice

Pineapples

The knobbly skin of the pineapple can vary in colour from pale to deep golden. Choose fruits with top leaves which are firm and crisp. Inside, the creamy white or golden flesh is sweet and juicy with a distinctive flavour, and can be eaten raw as a dessert fruit or used in cooking.

1 small pineapple

2 large oranges

3 × 15ml tbsp (3tbsp) water

2 × 15ml tbsp (2tbsp) caster sugar

2–3 × 15ml tbsp (2–3tbsp) kirsch

6 maraschino cherries

For decoration:
mint leaves

For serving:
cream

Pineapple and orange kirsch *(serves 6)*
POWER SETTING: NORMAL, FULL OR HIGH

1 Cut the pineapple into 6 slices. Cut away the skin and remove woody core from each slice.
2 Peel the oranges and remove all white pith and membrane. Cut each orange into 6 slices.
3 Arrange the pineapple in overlapping slices down the centre of an oval serving dish. Arrange a row of orange slices down each side of the pineapple.
4 Place the water and caster sugar into a small bowl, heat for 1½ min and stir until sugar is dissolved. Add the kirsch and spoon over the pineapple.
5 Arrange a maraschino cherry in the centre of each slice of pineapple and decorate with mint leaves.
6 Serve chilled with cream.

1 20cm (8in) baked flan case (page 112)

For the filling:
225g (8oz) cream cheese

50g (2oz) caster sugar

3 egg yolks, beaten

150ml (¼pt) chopped fresh or canned pineapple

For decoration:
toasted coconut

3 pineapple rings, fresh or canned

maraschino cherries

Pineapple cheese tart *(serves 6)*
POWER SETTING: DEFROST OR MEDIUM

1 Cream the cheese in a bowl with the sugar until soft. Beat in the egg yolks gradually, stir in the chopped pineapple.
2 Heat on defrost or medium setting for about 5 min, beating the mixture every minute, until thickened.
3 Pour into the flan case, smooth the top and allow to cool.
4 Sprinkle toasted coconut over the top of the flan.
5 Cut the pineapple rings into small wedges and arrange around the edge of the flan and decorate with a few maraschino cherries.
6 Serve warm or cold.

2 small fresh pineapples

sugar

275ml (½pt) pineapple juice

150ml (¼pt) water

225g (8oz) sugar

1 lemon, grated rind and juice

2–3 × 15ml tbsp (2–3tbsp) kirsch

275ml (½pt) double cream, whipped

*St Clementine Sorbet (page 89);
Frozen Pineapple Dessert (above)*

Frozen pineapple dessert *(serves 4)*
POWER SETTING: NORMAL, FULL OR HIGH

1 Cut the pineapples in half lengthways, leaving the green tops intact.
2 Carefully scoop out the flesh taking care not to break the skins. Discard the cores.
3 Sprinkle the pineapple skins with sugar, cover and chill in the refrigerator.
4 Chop the pineapple flesh finely and place in a bowl with the juice, water, sugar and lemon rind.
5 Bring to the boil in the microwave and cook uncovered for 5 min. Add the lemon juice and kirsch. Leave to cool before freezing.
6 Before it freezes too hard, beat or whisk in a mixer and fold in the whipped cream. Return to the freezer to harden.
7 Spoon the mixture into the chilled pineapple shells and serve immediately.

Plums

Both dessert and culinary varieties are available and vary in colour from yellow to dark blue. Dessert plums should be firm to the touch with a slight bloom on the skin. They ripen quickly at room temperature but store well in a cool larder or refrigerator. Greengages are a type of plum and are considered to have the best flavour. Damsons have dark blue-black skins and green flesh which is tart and sour.

Damson cobbler *(serves 4–6)*

POWER SETTING: NORMAL, FULL OR HIGH

Cobbler is a scone mix topping – delicious with blackcurrants too

675g (1½lb) damsons, washed
100–175g (4–6oz) sugar
100g (4oz) self-raising flour
100g (4oz) wholemeal flour
pinch salt
½ × 5ml tsp (½tsp) baking powder
50g (2oz) butter or margarine
25g (1oz) caster sugar
milk for mixing
caster sugar for sprinkling
For serving:
custard or cream

1 Place the damsons and the sugar in a bowl or casserole dish, cover with a lid and cook for 8–10 min until tender. Add a little more sugar to taste if necessary. Place the fruit in a 20cm (8in) round dish.
2 Mix the flours with the salt and baking powder. Rub in the butter or margarine finely. Stir in the sugar. Mix in sufficient milk to make a soft scone dough.
3 Roll out the dough on a lightly floured surface to 1.25cm (½in) thick. Cut into rounds with a 5cm (2in) cutter. Arrange the rounds over the fruit and brush with milk. Sprinkle with the sugar.
4 Cook for 5–6 min, turning the dish twice throughout.
5 Serve hot or cold with custard or cream.

Alternative conventional bake
Cook in a preheated oven at 200°C (400°F) Mark 6 for 20–25 min.

Sweet damson pickle *(makes about 1kg [2lb])*

POWER SETTING: DEFROST OR MEDIUM AND NORMAL, FULL OR HIGH

1kg (2lb) damsons, washed
rind of ½ lemon
6 cloves
6 allspice seeds
small piece each root ginger and cinnamon stick
450g (1lb) brown sugar
275ml (½pt) vinegar

1 Place the whole damsons in a large bowl. Tie the lemon rind and spices in a muslin bag and add to the damsons.
2 Dissolve the sugar in the vinegar and pour over the damsons.
3 Cover with a lid or clingfilm and cook on defrost or medium setting for 12–15 min until the damsons are tender.
4 Drain and pack the fruit neatly into warmed jars.
5 Boil the vinegar in the microwave on normal, full or high setting until it is reduced to a thin syrup. Remove muslin bag.
6 Pour over the fruit in the jars and seal and label immediately.

Plums with yoghurt *(serves 4)*

POWER SETTING: NORMAL, FULL OR HIGH AND DEFROST OR MEDIUM

450g (1lb) dessert plums
1 × 5ml tsp (1tsp) cinnamon
sugar to taste
2 egg yolks
275ml (½pt) natural yoghurt
25–50g (1–2oz) caster sugar
½ × 5ml tsp (½tsp) vanilla essence
2 × 15ml tbsp (2tbsp) chopped walnuts

1 Wash and halve the plums. Remove stones and place the fruit in a 17.5cm (7in) round dish. Mix the cinnamon with the sugar and sprinkle over the plums. Cover and cook for 4 min on normal, full or high setting, turning or stirring once throughout.
2 Beat the egg yolks with the yoghurt. Beat in the caster sugar and vanilla essence. Heat for 1½ min, whisking every 30 sec until heated through.
3 Pour the topping over the plums. Cook in the microwave on defrost or medium setting for 5 min until the topping is set.
4 Serve hot or cold sprinkled with the chopped walnuts.

DO NOT FREEZE THIS DISH.

Greengage charlotte with apricot purée *(serves 4)*
POWER SETTING: NORMAL, FULL OR HIGH

450g (1lb) greengages, washed
sugar to taste
75–100g (3–4oz) butter
6 slices white bread, crusts
removed
2 × 15ml tbsp (2tbsp)
demerara sugar
275ml (½pt) apricot purée
(page 29)

1 Cut the greengages in half and remove the stones. Place in a shallow dish and add sugar to taste. Cover and cook for 4 min, shaking or stirring once throughout.
2 Melt the butter for 2–3 min. Cut the bread slices into quarters and dip into the melted butter.
3 Preheat a browning dish for 5–6 min and cook half the bread for 1 min each side until lightly brown. Preheat the browning dish for a further 2–3 min and brown the remaining bread.
4 Arrange the toasted bread over the greengages and sprinkle with the demerara sugar.
5 Heat through for about 2 min and serve hot with apricot purée handed separately.

Alternative conventional bake
The bread slices may be dipped in butter and then fried in a frying pan before arranging over the fruit and heating through in the microwave cooker. Alternatively, arrange the buttered bread slices over the fruit and cook in a preheated oven at 190°C (375°F) Mark 5 for 35–40 min until crisp and brown.

Plums in wine *(serves 4–6)*
POWER SETTING: DEFROST OR MEDIUM AND NORMAL, FULL OR HIGH

675g (1½lb) dessert plums
100–175g (4–6oz) caster sugar
275ml (½pt) boiling water
275ml (½pt) port or red wine
1 orange, grated rind
sugar to taste
25g (1oz) flaked almonds,
toasted
For serving:
cream

1 Wash the plums and prick each one once with a fork. Sprinkle with 100–175g (4–6oz) caster sugar and cook in a covered dish on defrost or medium setting for 8–10 min until just tender. Shake or stir gently twice throughout.
2 Mix the boiling water with the port or red wine in a large bowl or jug. Stir in the orange rind and bring to the boil in the microwave.
3 Pour the water and wine over the cooked plums and allow to stand for 10 min.
4 Remove the plums from the wine with a slotted spoon and place in a serving dish.
5 Add extra sugar to taste to the wine. Bring back to the boil in the microwave and boil until reduced by a third. Pour over the plums.
6 Scatter the almonds over the top of the dish and serve hot with cream.

For the suet crust:
175g (6oz) self-raising flour
pinch salt
50g (2oz) fresh white
breadcrumbs
100g (4oz) shredded suet
150ml (¼pt) cold water,
approximately
For the filling:
675–900g (1½–2lb) plums or
greengages, halved and stoned
100g (4oz) caster sugar,
approximately
For serving:
custard or cream

Plum pudding *(serves 6–8)*
POWER SETTING: NORMAL, FULL OR HIGH

This suet pudding may be filled with plums or greengages

1 Sift the flour and salt. Stir in the breadcrumbs and suet. Mix to a soft, manageable dough with the water.
2 Roll out two-thirds of the pastry on a floured surface and line a 1¼l (2pt) pudding basin.
3 Layer the fruit and sugar into the lined basin. Roll out the remaining pastry to fit the top of the pudding, dampen and seal the edges.
4 Cover the top of the basin very tightly with clingfilm.
5 Turn the basin upside down on the microwave cooker shelf or on a plate and cook for 5 min.
6 Turn the pudding the right way up and cook for 5 min. Remove clingfilm and cook for a further 1–2 min.
7 Allow to stand for 10 min before inverting onto a serving plate.
8 Serve hot with custard or cream.

Alternative conventional bake
Cover the basin with greased greaseproof paper and then securely with aluminium foil. Place in a steamer over a pan of gently boiling water and steam for 2½–3 hours.

Potatoes

The wide varieties of potatoes available throughout the year are popular due to their versatility in cooking and the fact that they are relatively inexpensive. In the microwave, potatoes are best cooked in their skins and then peeled if required, as some varieties tend not to cook well if peeled before cooking.

450g (1lb) potatoes, washed
2 × 15ml tbsp (2tbsp) salted
water
75–125ml (3–4fl oz) milk
25g (1oz) butter
salt and pepper

Creamed potatoes *(serves 4)*   colour page 35
POWER SETTING: NORMAL, FULL OR HIGH

1 Prick the skins of the potatoes with a fork. Place with the salted water in a casserole dish, cover and cook for 10–12 min until tender. Test with a fork.
2 Drain the potatoes, remove the skins or cut in half and scoop out the potato from the skins.
3 Mash the potatoes with a fork or potato masher.
4 Heat the milk for 1 min and add to the potatoes with the butter and seasoning.
5 Beat well together and serve hot.

Almondine potatoes

Follow the method and ingredients for creamed potatoes, omitting the milk but stirring in the butter and seasonings to taste. Allow the mixture to cool then refrigerate until cold. Divide the mixture into 8 portions and roll into balls, shaped between the palms of the hands, using a little flour if necessary to prevent the potatoes from sticking. Roll the potato balls in finely chopped and toasted almonds. Place on the microwave cooker shelf or in a serving dish and heat through uncovered for about 3 min.

Almondine Potatoes (above); Creamed Mushrooms and Peas (page 81)

Sauté potatoes

Cook 450g (1lb) potatoes in their jackets for 10–12 min. When cooked, allow to cool, then remove the skins carefully and cut the potatoes into thick slices. Heat 1 × 15ml tbsp (1tbsp) each of butter and oil for 1–2 min and brush over the potato slices. Preheat a browning dish for 6–8 min, depending on size, then toss in the potatoes. Cover and cook for 3–4 min, turning the potatoes over twice throughout so that they are evenly browned. Serve hot sprinkled with a little paprika pepper.

Lyonnaise potatoes

Cook some sauté potatoes as given above and, when finished, stir in a few fried onions (page 86). Cover and heat through before serving.

Potato and tuna bake (serves 4)
POWER SETTING: NORMAL, FULL OR HIGH AND DEFROST OR MEDIUM

675g (1½lb) potatoes, washed
2 × 15ml tbsp (2tbsp) oil
1 large onion, peeled and sliced
1 clove garlic, crushed
425g (15oz) can tomatoes
1 × 5ml tsp (1tsp) dried mixed herbs
salt and freshly ground black pepper
200g (7oz) can tuna fish, drained and flaked
75g (3oz) cheddar cheese, grated
For serving:
crusty french bread or garlic bread

1 Prick the skins of the potatoes with a fork and cook in the microwave for 10–12 min on normal, full or high setting.
2 Carefully remove the skins and cut the potatoes into dice.
3 Place the oil in a large bowl, toss in the onion and garlic, cover and cook on normal, full or high setting for 5–6 min. Stir in the tomatoes, herbs and seasoning to taste.
4 Layer the potato, tuna fish and tomato mixture in a 20cm (8in) round casserole, starting with a layer of potato and ending with a layer of tomato.
5 Cover and cook on normal, full or high setting for 5 min, then reduce to defrost or medium setting for 15–20 min until the potatoes are tender. Allow to stand for 5 min.
6 Sprinkle with the grated cheese, cook on normal, full or high setting for 2–3 min to melt the cheese. Alternatively, brown under a hot grill.
7 Serve hot with crusty french bread or garlic bread.

Potatoes duxelles (serves 4)   colour page 15
POWER SETTING: NORMAL, FULL OR HIGH

450g (1lb) small, new potatoes, washed
2 × 15ml tbsp (2tbsp) salted water
For the sauce:
15g (½oz) butter
2 × 5ml tsp (2tsp) finely chopped onion
100g (4oz) mushrooms, washed and finely chopped
15g (½oz) flour
175ml (6fl oz) chicken stock
salt and pepper
1 bay leaf
For garnish:
chopped mint

1 Place the potatoes and salted water in a covered casserole dish and cook for 10–12 min, stirring twice throughout. Leave to stand for a few minutes.
2 Melt the butter in a bowl or jug for 30 sec. Stir in the onion, cover and cook for 1 min. Add the mushrooms and toss well in the onion and butter. Cover and cook for 3 min.
3 Stir in the flour, then pour in the stock, seasonings and bay leaf. Bring to the boil in the microwave, stirring every minute until thickened; continue to cook for 1 min.
4 Drain the potatoes and remove the skins. Remove the bay leaf from the sauce and stir in the potatoes.
5 Serve hot, sprinkled with chopped mint.

Note: *Canned new potatoes may be used for this dish if fresh new potatoes are not available.*

DO NOT FREEZE THIS DISH.

Quinces

These round or pear-shaped fruits are principally used in jams, jellies and for flavouring in pies. They are sometimes available in the shops during October and November. The tough skin is golden when ripe whilst the acid, aromatic flesh remains firm.

Quince and apple sauce *(makes about 275ml [½pt])*
POWER SETTING: NORMAL, FULL OR HIGH

Serve with rich roast meats and poultry, ie pork, duck or goose

1 Place the sliced quinces in a bowl with half the cider or water and the sugar. Cover and cook for 6–7 min until tender.
2 Put the apples with the rest of the cider or water and rind into a bowl, cover and cook for 4–5 min until tender. Rub the apples through a sieve.
3 Combine the apple purée with the quinces and season lightly. Stir in the butter and cook uncovered until thick, 2–3 min.
4 Serve hot or cold with pork, duck or goose.

2 small quinces, peeled, cored and thinly sliced
150ml (¼pt) cider or water
2 × 15ml tbsp (2tbsp) sugar
225g (8oz) red apples, cored and thinly sliced
strip lemon rind
salt and pepper
15g (½oz) butter

Quince jelly *(makes about 1¾kg [3½lb])*
POWER SETTING: NORMAL, FULL OR HIGH

1 Cut the quinces into small pieces and place in a large bowl with sufficient hot water to barely cover the fruit. Cover and cook for 12–15 min until tender.
2 Put the fruit and water through a jelly bag or cloth and measure the extract. You will need 450g (1lb) sugar for every 550ml (1pt) juice.
3 Stir the sugar into the extract and continue to stir until dissolved. If necessary, heat for 2–3 min at a time to boost the temperature of the extract.
4 Add the pared lemon rind and the lemon juice and cook uncovered in the microwave until setting point is reached, about 35–40 min.
5 Remove the lemon rind, pour into warm jars, seal and label.

1½kg (3lb) unripe quinces, washed
825ml (1½pt) hot water, approximately
675g (1½lb) preserving sugar, approximately
1 lemon, pared rind and juice

Note: *If ripe quinces are used, commercial pectin or 6g (¼oz) citric acid may be required to assist with the setting of the jelly.*

Raspberries

This popular soft fruit should be used as soon as possible after purchasing as raspberries can deteriorate very quickly. The season is short, but frozen raspberries are widely available and can be used in a variety of dishes.

Raspberry and apple pudding (serves 4–6)
POWER SETTING: NORMAL, FULL OR HIGH

For the suet crust:
225g (8oz) self-raising flour
175g (6oz) shredded suet
water to mix
For the filling:
450g (1lb) raspberries
450g (1lb) cooking apples, peeled, cored and sliced
100g (4oz) caster sugar
For serving:
custard or cream

1 Place the flour and suet together in a mixing bowl. Mix to a soft manageable dough with cold water.
2 Lightly grease an 850ml (1½pt) pudding basin and line with two-thirds of the suet pastry.
3 Layer the filling into the lined basin. Roll out the remaining pastry to a circle to fit the top of the pudding. Dampen and seal the edges.
4 Cover the top of the basin very tightly with clingfilm. Invert the basin and cook in the microwave for 2 min.
5 Place the pudding the right way up and cook for 5 min. Remove the clingfilm, turn the basin and cook for a further 5 min. Allow to stand for a few minutes.
6 Turn the pudding onto a serving plate or dish and serve hot with custard or cream.

Raspberry mousse (serves 4)
POWER SETTING: NORMAL, FULL OR HIGH

275ml (½pt) raspberry purée (see below)
2–3 × 15ml tbsp (2–3tbsp) caster sugar
150ml (¼pt) double cream
3 × 15ml tbsp (3 tbsp) raspberry juice or water
15g (½oz) gelatine
2 egg whites, whisked
For decoration:
whipped cream

1 Place the raspberry purée into a mixing bowl and stir in the caster sugar to taste.
2 Whip the double cream and fold into the raspberry purée.
3 Place the raspberry juice or water into a small bowl or jug and sprinkle on the gelatine.
4 Heat for 15–30 sec and stir until the gelatine is dissolved completely, then allow to cool slightly.
5 Pour the gelatine into the raspberry mixture in a steady stream, stirring the mixture all the time.
6 Fold in the whisked egg whites carefully with a metal spoon, cutting and turning until the mixture is smooth.
7 Pour into a serving dish or into individual serving glasses.
8 Chill before serving piped with whipped cream.

Note: *2 × 425g (15oz) cans raspberries, drained or 450g (1lb) fresh or frozen raspberries sieved or blended in a liquidiser or food processor will make 275ml (½pt) purée.*

Rhubarb Chutney (page 110); Creamy Rhubarb and Ginger Flan (page 109); Rhubarb and Ginger Compôte (page 109)

450g (1lb) raspberries, washed
50g (2oz) caster sugar
100g (4oz) porridge oats
425ml (¾pt) double or whipping cream
25g (1oz) icing sugar, sieved
50g (2oz) chopped nuts

Raspberry oat sundaes (serves 6)
POWER SETTING: NORMAL, FULL OR HIGH

1 Reserve some raspberries for decoration, cook the remainder with the caster sugar for 4 min.
2 'Toast' the oats by placing on a plate and cooking for 3 min in the microwave, stirring or tossing them over every minute. Leave to cool.
3 Whip the cream and reserve a third for decoration. Fold in the icing sugar. Reserving a few of the chopped nuts, fold the rest into the cream with the oats.
4 Divide the raspberries between individual serving glasses and top with the oat and cream mixture. Decorate with the remaining whipped cream, nuts and raspberries and serve immediately.

DO NOT FREEZE THIS DISH.

3 eggs, separated
75g (3oz) caster sugar
1 × 15ml tbsp (1tbsp) lemon juice
4 × 15ml tbsp (4tbsp) raspberry juice or water
15g (½oz) gelatine
75ml (2½fl oz) raspberry purée (page 106)
75ml (2½fl oz) double cream, whipped
For decoration:
finely chopped nuts
whipped double cream

Raspberry soufflé (serves 4–6)   colour page 15
POWER SETTING: NORMAL, FULL OR HIGH

Strawberries or apricots can be used for this light but rich special dessert

1 Prepare a 12.5cm (5in) soufflé dish (see below).
2 Place the egg yolks with the caster sugar, lemon juice and 2 × 15ml tbsp (2tbsp) of the fruit juice or water into a large bowl.
3 Whisk until very thick and creamy and the mixture leaves a trail over the surface from the whisk. If a food mixer is not available, stand the bowl over a pan of hot water which helps to thicken the mixture during whisking. Continue to whisk until the mixture is cool.
4 Place the rest of the fruit juice or water into a small bowl and sprinkle in the gelatine. Heat in the microwave for 15–30 sec and then stir until dissolved. Allow to cool slightly.
5 Pour the gelatine onto the whisked mixture in a thin stream, stirring all the time.
6 Fold in the fruit purée and the whipped cream.
7 Whisk the egg whites until stiff and fold in with a metal spoon, cutting and turning the mixture carefully until it is smooth. Take care not to overmix otherwise the soufflé will become flat.
8 Pour the mixture into the prepared soufflé dish and leave to chill in the refrigerator.
9 When set, carefully remove the band of paper from the dish and ease it from the soufflé with a knife dipped in hot water.
10 Press chopped nuts into the sides of the soufflé and decorate with piped whipped cream. Serve chilled.

Note: *To prepare the soufflé dish, measure a band of double greaseproof paper around the whole depth of the outside of the dish so that it stands 7.5cm (3in) above the rim. Tie firmly with string so that the paper fits closely to the rim of the dish. This will prevent any mixture escaping when poured in to about 2.5cm (1in) above the rim.*

Rhubarb

Although used as a fruit, the plant is in fact a vegetable. The tart stems are used in a variety of recipes and are poached or stewed with sugar before eating. Choose firm, crisp stalks and discard the leaves. Forced rhubarb is tender and pale pink in colour, and is available from late December to March. Maincrop rhubarb is darker in colour with stronger flavour, and is available from March to June.

Creamy rhubarb and ginger flan (*serves 6–8*)   *colour page 107*
POWER SETTING: NORMAL, FULL OR HIGH

1 Wash and trim the rhubarb and cut into 2.5cm (1in) lengths. Place with the syrup in a covered casserole, roasting or boiling bag and cook for 5–6 min until tender.
2 Melt the butter for 2–3 min, stir in the biscuit crumbs. Mix well together and press over the base and around the sides of a 20–22.5cm (8–9in) flan dish.
3 Blend the custard powder, ginger and caster sugar with the milk and cook for 2–3 min until thick, stirring every minute. When cool, beat in the cream.
4 Drain off some of the juice from the rhubarb and combine rhubarb with the custard and cream. The mixture may be blended in a liquidiser or sieved if preferred.
5 Pour into the biscuit base and leave until cold and set. Chill before serving and pipe with whipped cream.

DO NOT FREEZE THIS DISH.

450g (1lb) rhubarb
2–3 × 15ml tbsp (2–3tbsp) golden syrup
175g (6oz) butter
350g (12oz) ginger biscuits, crumbed
1½ × 15ml tbsp (1½tbsp) custard powder
1 × 5ml tsp (1tsp) ground ginger
2 × 5ml tsp (2tsp) caster sugar
150ml (¼pt) milk
150ml (¼pt) double or soured cream
For decoration:
whipped cream

Rhubarb and ginger compôte (*serves 4*)   *colour page 107*
POWER SETTING: NORMAL, FULL OR HIGH

1 Place the hot water and sugar in a serving bowl, stir until the sugar is dissolved. Bring to the boil in the microwave and cook uncovered for 5 min.
2 Add the ginger syrup *or* ground ginger, blended with a little of the hot syrup. Stir well and add the prepared rhubarb. Cover and cook for 7–10 min, shaking or stirring gently twice throughout.
3 Scatter the finely chopped preserved ginger over the rhubarb and chill before serving with sponge fingers and cream.

200ml (7fl oz) hot water
100g (4oz) sugar
2 × 15ml tbsp (2tbsp) ginger syrup *or*
½ × 5ml tsp (½tsp) ground ginger
450g (1lb) rhubarb, trimmed and cut into 3.75cm (1½in) lengths
2 × 15ml tbsp (2tbsp) finely chopped preserved ginger
For serving:
sponge fingers and cream

1¼kg (2½lb) rhubarb, washed and cut into small pieces

225g (8oz) onions, peeled and finely chopped or minced

450g (1lb) sugar

6g (¼oz) ground ginger

25g (1oz) ground mixed spice

6g (¼oz) salt

425ml (¾pt) vinegar

Rhubarb chutney *(makes about 1½–2kg [3–4lb])* *colour page 107*
POWER SETTING: NORMAL, FULL OR HIGH

1 Place the rhubarb, onions, sugar, spices and salt in a large bowl. Stir in 150ml (¼pt) of the vinegar.
2 Cover and cook for about 15 min, stirring every 5 min, until the rhubarb is tender.
3 Stir in the rest of the vinegar and cook uncovered until thick.
4 Pot, seal and label.

Spinach

This tender, green-leaved vegetable bruises easily and must be handled with care. Remove and discard any yellow or damaged leaves before washing several times in cold water; it is not normally necessary to add any extra water to the leaves when cooking. Spinach has a distinctive flavour and is dark green in appearance when cooked.

225g (8oz) tagliatelle

25g (1oz) butter or margarine

1 small onion, peeled and finely chopped

450g (1lb) frozen spinach, thawed

150ml (¼pt) single cream

salt and freshly ground black pepper

100g (4oz) cheddar cheese, finely grated

25g (1oz) fresh white breadcrumbs

15g (½oz) butter

grated parmesan cheese for sprinkling, optional

grated nutmeg for sprinkling

Spinach gratinée *(serves 4)* *colour page 80*
POWER SETTING: NORMAL, FULL OR HIGH

1 Cook the tagliatelle in boiling, salted water as given on page 20 and drain well.
2 Melt 25g (1oz) butter in a large bowl for 1 min, add the onion, cover and cook for 2 min.
3 Add the spinach and heat through for 3 min. Stir in the cream and salt and pepper to taste.
4 Arrange layers of the tagliatelle, spinach and finely grated cheddar cheese in a serving dish.
5 Cover and heat through for 5–6 min. Scatter on the fresh white breadcrumbs, dot with the 15g (½oz) butter and sprinkle with the parmesan cheese.
6 Cook uncovered for 2–3 min until the butter is melted or alternatively, brown under a hot grill.
7 Serve hot, sprinkled with grated nutmeg.

1 17.5cm (7in) baked flan case (page 112)

For the filling:
1 small onion, peeled and chopped

225g (8oz) cream cheese

2 egg yolks

225g (8oz) cooked fresh or frozen spinach, chopped

salt and pepper

Spinach Cheese Tart (above); Spinach Pudding with Tomato Sauce (page 112 and 114)

Spinach cheese tart *(serves 4–6)*
POWER SETTING: NORMAL, FULL OR HIGH AND DEFROST OR MEDIUM

1 Place the onion in a small dish, cover with clingfilm or a lid and cook for 2 min on normal, full or high setting.
2 Cream the cheese until soft, then add the egg yolks, beating well together.
3 Stir in the onion, spinach and salt and pepper to taste.
4 Spoon the mixture into the precooked flan case and cook on defrost or medium setting for 12–14 min until the filling is set.
5 Serve hot or cold.

Alternative conventional bake
When the filling is added to the flan case, cook in a preheated oven at 180°C (350°F) Mark 4 for 20–25 min until set.

350g (12oz) cooked, fresh or frozen spinach, finely chopped

75g (3oz) fresh white breadcrumbs

$\frac{1}{2}$ × 5ml tsp ($\frac{1}{2}$tsp) grated nutmeg

1 lemon, grated rind

salt and freshly ground black pepper

25g (1oz) butter or margarine

2 × 15ml tbsp (2tbsp) cream

2 eggs, beaten

For serving:
tomato sauce (page 114)

Spinach pudding (*serves 3–4*)   *colour page 111*
POWER SETTING: NORMAL, FULL OR HIGH

1 Lightly grease an 850ml (1$\frac{1}{2}$pt) pudding basin.
2 Mix together the spinach, breadcrumbs, nutmeg, lemon rind and seasoning to taste.
3 Melt the butter or margarine for 1 min and stir into the spinach mixture with the cream.
4 Add the beaten eggs and mix well together.
5 Place the mixture into the prepared pudding basin, cover with clingfilm and slit with the pointed end of a sharp knife.
6 Cook for 4–5 min, turning once halfway through. Remove clingfilm and invert onto a serving dish.
7 Serve hot with tomato sauce.

Strawberries

Strawberries are probably the most popular of all the soft fruits and during their short summer season are most often served as dessert fruits with cream and sugar. Although best eaten on the day they are bought, strawberries store quite well for one or two days in the refrigerator and can be used for a variety of dishes including cakes, tarts, ice creams, sorbets and jams. Strawberries frozen whole are best used in cooked dishes, otherwise freeze as a purée.

1 × 20cm (8in) baked flan case (below)

175g (6oz) cream cheese

50g (2oz) caster sugar

3 × 15ml tbsp (3tbsp) double or soured cream

450g (1lb) strawberries

2–3 × 15ml tbsp (2–3tbsp) redcurrant jelly

Strawberry cream flan (*serves 6–8*)   *colour page 19*
POWER SETTING: NORMAL, FULL OR HIGH

1 Place the cooked flan case on a large serving plate or in its flan dish.
2 Cream the cheese with the sugar, beating well together until light and fluffy. Beat in the cream.
3 Wash and dry the strawberries, heat the redcurrant jelly for $\frac{1}{2}$–1 min until melted.
4 Spread the cream cheese mixture in the base of the flan case. Arrange the strawberries over the top and brush with the warm glaze.
5 Serve when cooled and set.

DO NOT FREEZE THE FLAN WITH THE STRAWBERRIES. FINISH AND DECORATE JUST BEFORE SERVING.

150g (6oz) plain flour

pinch salt

75g (3oz) butter or margarine

2 × 5ml tsp (2tsp) caster sugar, optional

1 egg yolk

2 × 15ml tbsp (2tbsp) water

Flan case: rich shortcrust pastry (*for a 20cm [8in] flan case*)
POWER SETTING: NORMAL, FULL OR HIGH

1 Sift the flour with the salt and rub in the butter or margarine finely. Stir in the sugar if used.
2 Beat the egg yolk with the water and add the flour. Mix well together, then knead together lightly.
3 Chill before rolling out.

To line a flan dish:
Roll out the pastry into a circle 5cm (2in) larger than the dish. Wrap the pastry loosely round the rolling pin and lift into the flan ring. Ease the pastry into shape removing any air from under the base, pressing well into the sides and taking care not to stretch the pastry. Cut the pastry away but leave 6mm (¼in) above the rim of the flan dish. Carefully ease this down into the dish, or flute the edges and leave slightly higher than the rim of the dish (this allows a little extra height to the sides of the flan case to allow for any shrinkage during cooking). Alternatively, roll the rolling pin across the top of the flan to cut off the surplus pastry. Prick the base well with a fork.

To bake blind:
Using a long, smooth strip of aluminium foil measuring approximately 3.75cm (1½in) wide, line the inside, upright edge of the pastry flan case. This protects the edges from overcooking in the microwave. Place two pieces of absorbent kitchen paper over the base, easing around the edges and pressing gently into the corners to help to keep the foil strip in position. Place in the microwave and cook for 4–4½ min on power setting full or high, giving the dish a quarter turn every minute. Remove the kitchen paper and foil and cook for a further 1–2 min.

Alternative conventional bake:
Line the pastry flan case with a circle of lightly greased greaseproof paper (greased side down) or kitchen paper. Half fill the paper with uncooked beans, lentils, small pasta or rice which may be specially kept for this purpose. Alternatively, line the pastry flan case with foil only. Cook in a preheated oven at 200°C (400°F) Mark 6 for 15–20 min, until the pastry is nearly cooked. Remove lining and bake for 5–10 min until the base is firm and dry.

Note: *For savoury dishes, half the plain flour may be replaced by wholemeal flour, and omit the sugar from the pastry ingredients.*

Strawberry ice cream *(serves 4–5)* *colour page 19*
POWER SETTING: NORMAL, FULL OR HIGH

3 eggs, beaten
275ml (½pt) single cream
100g (4oz) caster sugar
275ml (½pt) double cream, lightly whipped
225g (8oz) strawberries, puréed

1 Place eggs, single cream and sugar in a bowl and whisk well together.
2 Heat in the microwave for approximately 5 min, whisking every 30 sec. Do not allow the mixture to boil.
3 Cool quickly over a bowl of iced water. Pour into a container and freeze until the edge is frozen.
4 Place the mixture into a bowl and beat well.
5 Fold in the double cream. Trickle the purée into the mixture and fold in lightly.
6 Place back into the container and return to the freezer until the ice cream is set.

Strawberry jam *(makes about 1½kg [3lb])*
POWER SETTING: NORMAL, FULL OR HIGH

1¾kg (3½lb) strawberries, hulled and washed
15g (½oz) citric acid
1¼kg (2¾lb) preserving sugar

1 Place the strawberries in a large glass bowl. Sprinkle with the citric acid and cook for about 15 min until soft.
2 Add the sugar and stir well. Cook the jam, uncovered, for 40 min or until setting point is reached. Stir the jam every 10 min at the beginning of cooking and every 5 min towards the end of the time.
3 Allow the jam to stand for 20–30 min. Pour into warm jars, seal and label.

Swedes

This winter root vegetable is similar to the turnip but the flesh is yellow in appearance and milder in flavour. Swedes may be cooked in butter, or creamed in the same way as parsnips (page 92).

Tomatoes

Although imported tomatoes are available all the year round, those with the best flavour are home grown. Tomatoes should be regular in shape and avoid any with damaged or soft skins. Ripe but firm tomatoes are best for salads and the large orange/red ones are good for stuffing.

Tomatoes may be skinned more easily by first heating in the microwave cooker – 4 tomatoes require about 1½ min.

1 × 15ml tbsp (1tbsp) olive oil

1 large onion, peeled and finely chopped

1–2 cloves garlic, crushed or finely chopped

400g (14oz) can tomatoes, drained

1 × 15ml tbsp (1tbsp) tomato purée

1 glass red wine or juice from tomatoes

few sprigs of fresh herbs *or*

1 × 5ml tsp (1tsp) dried herbs, eg thyme or rosemary

salt and freshly ground black pepper

Tomato sauce *(makes about 275ml [½pt])*   *colour page 111*
POWER SETTING: NORMAL, FULL OR HIGH

1 Place olive oil, onion and garlic into a bowl and toss well. Cook for 4–5 min until soft.
2 Roughly chop the tomatoes and add to the bowl with the remaining ingredients.
3 Cook uncovered until soft and the liquid quantity is reduced giving a fairly thick sauce, stirring every 3 min.
4 Use when referred to in recipes or where a good, well-flavoured tomato sauce is required, ie as a topping for pizzas or to mix with plainly boiled pasta.

550ml (1pt) tomato sauce (see above)

225g (8oz) mushrooms, washed and sliced

75g (3oz) wholemeal flour

75g (3oz) plain flour

½ × 5ml tsp (½tsp) salt

½ × 5ml tsp (½tsp) dry mustard

75g (3oz) butter or margarine

75g (3oz) cheese, finely grated

For garnish:
tomato slices

Tomato and Mushroom Crumble (above); Baked Stuffed Tomatoes (page 116)

Tomato and mushroom crumble *(serves 4–6)*
POWER SETTING: NORMAL, FULL OR HIGH

1 Lightly grease a large round ovenware dish.
2 Mix the tomato sauce with the sliced mushrooms and place in the greased dish.
3 Sift the flours with the salt and mustard and rub in the butter or margarine finely. Stir in the grated cheese.
4 Sprinkle the crumble topping lightly over the tomato mixture and smooth the top.
5 Cook for 8–10 min, giving a quarter turn every 2 min until hot through and the crumble is cooked.
6 Serve hot garnished with tomato slices.

Alternative conventional bake:
Cook in a preheated oven at 190°C (375°F) Mark 5 for 40–45 min.

40g (1½oz) butter

40g (1½oz) flour

425ml (¾pt) milk

salt and freshly ground black pepper

100g (4oz) gruyère cheese, grated

4 × 15ml tbsp (4tbsp) single cream or top of the milk

675g (1½lb) firm tomatoes, skinned and sliced

1 × 5ml tsp (1tsp) dried basil

2 × 5ml tsp (2tsp) caster sugar

25g (1oz) grated parmesan cheese

For garnish:
chopped parsley or paprika pepper

Swiss tomato casserole *(serves 4–6)*
POWER SETTING: NORMAL, FULL OR HIGH

1 Melt the butter in a bowl for 1½ min. Stir in the flour and add the milk gradually, beating well until smooth.
2 Heat for 5–6 min until the sauce is thickened and bubbling, stirring every minute. Season to taste and stir in the cheese and cream or milk.
3 Arrange a layer of tomatoes in the bottom of a casserole dish. Sprinkle with seasoning, a little basil and sugar. Spoon some of the sauce over the tomatoes.
4 Continue with the layers until all the ingredients are used, finishing with a layer of sauce.
5 Sprinkle with parmesan cheese, cover and cook for 10–12 min.
6 Serve hot, sprinkled with chopped parsley or paprika pepper.

12 large, firm tomatoes

40g (1½oz) butter or margarine

1 onion, peeled and finely chopped

175g (6oz) cooked meat, minced

100g (4oz) cooked rice

1 × 15ml tbsp (1tbsp) single cream or top of the milk

2 × 5ml tsp (2tsp) worcestershire sauce

2 × 15ml tbsp (2tbsp) chopped parsley

salt and freshly ground black pepper

50g (2oz) cheese, grated

1 × 15ml tbsp (1tbsp) fresh breadcrumbs

For garnish:
sprigs of parsley

Baked stuffed tomatoes *(serves 6)* colour page 115
POWER SETTING: NORMAL, FULL OR HIGH

Serve as a starter or as a main course with vegetables or rice

1 Cut a thin slice from the top of each tomato and scoop out the flesh.
2 Melt the butter or margarine in a bowl for 1½ min, toss in the onion and cook for 3–4 min.
3 Stir in the meat, rice, cream or top of the milk, worcestershire sauce and the parsley. Season to taste.
4 Fill the tomato cases with the meat mixture and place in a shallow, round serving dish.
5 Cover and cook for 4–5 min until heated through.
6 Mix together the cheese and breadcrumbs and sprinkle over the top of the tomatoes. Cook uncovered for 1½–2 min until the cheese is melted.
7 Serve hot, garnished with parsley sprigs.

Turnips

Early turnips are available from April to July and can be purchased in bunches. They have an excellent flavour and can be eaten either raw or cooked. Maincrop turnips are in the shops during autumn and winter and usually have a coarser texture. Although turnips are known primarily as a root vegetable, turnip tops may also be cooked and served in a similar way to spinach.

Cream of turnip soup *(serves 6)*
POWER SETTING: NORMAL, FULL OR HIGH

Use early turnips for this delicious vegetable soup

1 Melt the butter in a large bowl for 1½–2 min. Add all the vegetables, toss well in the butter. Cover and cook for 12–15 min, shaking or stirring every 5 min.
2 Stir in the flour and blend in the boiling stock. Season to taste.
3 Cook for 15–20 min until the vegetables are tender. Purée the soup in a liquidiser or pass through a sieve.
4 Beat the egg yolks with the cream, add a little of the soup and stir until well blended. Add this to the soup and mix well. Adjust seasoning.
5 Heat without boiling. Serve hot, garnished with croûtons or hand them separately.

50g (2oz) butter
350g (12oz) young turnips, peeled and diced
225g (8oz) potatoes, peeled and diced
1 leek, trimmed, washed and chopped
1 onion, peeled and chopped
25g (1oz) flour
2l (3½pt) boiling chicken or vegetable stock
salt and freshly ground black pepper
2 egg yolks
3 × 15ml tbsp (3tbsp) double cream
For garnish:
croûtons

Turnips with onions *(serves 4)*
POWER SETTING: NORMAL, FULL OR HIGH

1 Cut the turnips into 6mm (¼in) slices. Place in a roasting bag or casserole dish with the salted water, cover and cook for 8–10 min until tender, shaking or stirring halfway through. Drain well.
2 Slice the onions into thin rings. Melt the butter for 1½ min, add the onions and seasoning and toss over well. Cover and cook for 8–9 min, stirring twice throughout.
3 Mix together the turnips and onions and serve hot, sprinkled with a little extra ground black pepper.

450g (1lb) small turnips, peeled
2 × 15ml tbsp (2tbsp) salted water
450g (1lb) medium onions, peeled
40g (1½oz) butter
salt and freshly ground black pepper

Glazed turnips *(serves 4)* *colour page 15*
POWER SETTING: NORMAL, FULL OR HIGH

1 Place the turnips with the salted water in a casserole dish. Cover and cook for about 10 min until tender.
2 Drain off the water and add the butter, pepper and caster sugar. Toss over well until the butter is melted.
3 Cook uncovered for 3–4 min until any remaining moisture has evaporated, leaving the butter and sugar glaze around the turnips. Stir or shake the dish frequently.
4 Stir in the chopped parsley and serve hot.

450g (1lb) small whole turnips, peeled
4 × 15ml tbsp (4tbsp) salted water
25g (1oz) butter
freshly ground black pepper
1 × 5ml tsp (1tsp) caster sugar
1 × 15ml tbsp (1tbsp) chopped parsley

Index

Numbers in italics refer to illustrations

Courgettes Maison (page 63); Apricot and Almond Pudding with Apricot Purée (page 28)